MAD COW

MAD COW
A PTSD Love Story

Meredith Shafer

Mad Cow: A PTSD Love Story

Cover design by Samson Lim
Interior design by Gram Telen

Published in the United States of America

ISBN: 978-1543120059
1. Biography & Autobiography / Personal Memoirs
2. Religion / Christian Life / Family

This book is dedicated to Mr. Wonderful and my Traveling Circus, and to all veterans past and present. My family thanks you for your service.

Acknowledgements

Nothing in my life is possible without my Jesus. He is my healer, my hope, my friend, and my redeemer. Without him, I would have a lot of blank pages.

Mr. Wonderful—you keep going even when it seems impossible, and your lion-heartedness shines through everything you do for our family. Thank you for always bringing me coffee, for taking me on date nights, for showing our kids how to persevere even through dark days. Thank you for having my back, for your love, and for your unwavering support of my dreams. You are my hero, and I believe our best is yet to come.

To my Traveling Circus—I never dreamed I would be the mama of four! I'm blessed beyond measure that God gave each one of you to me, that you are following Jesus with your hearts, that you each contribute something special and amazing to this family. Thanks for making me laugh and interrupting my writing time to keep me humble and my priorities straight.

To the friends and family who loved us through 2013—there are no words. I'm humbled by your generosity and love and how you showed Jesus to us every day.

To my Prayer Warriors—you know who you are—thank you for covering me and my family daily and allowing me to do the same for you. Your prayers are invaluable and you ladies are dangerous!

Finally, to all veterans who suffer from PTSD and to your caregivers—we get you. We support you. We love you and we will not stop telling our story until everyone gets the care they deserve. There may still be hard days ahead, but please don't quit. You are not alone and your story isn't over yet.

....

To connect with Meredith Shafer, get more information, or have her tell her story, go to www.meredithshafer.com.

Contents

Bent: The End of Our Beginning

It's probably good that I didn't see the shotgun right away.

If I had, our story may have turned out differently. As I approached my husband, all I could think was, *How did we get here?*

Well, that and, *Jesus save us.*

Lifetimes passed in those first minutes. I heard my every heartbeat pound in my ears and the rapid breathing in my chest. Birds were singing ridiculous, carefree songs in the trees. The sunshine pouring into the doorway of that small space felt absurd. I was trying to wrap my mind around what was happening when I had the sudden realization that I was fighting for more minutes. And for my husband's life.

But I'm getting a little ahead of myself.

My family's story had been rather fairytale-ish up to this point. We lived a messy modern-day love story at the beginning of our beginning. I was remarried to a handsome prince, my soul mate, a man I call Mr. Wonderful. When he married me, he got a ready-made family consisting of two boys whom I had adopted with my ex-husband. My 6'6", 330 pound army guy didn't waver at this; instead, he opened his giant-sized heart to my boys as well. He turned out to be an amazing stepdad, which was good news since we found out we were pregnant about fifteen minutes after we got married. We became a party of five. Mr. Wonderful got militarily promoted to sergeant first class, and I enjoyed my job executive directing at the Wegener Foundation. We moved to the country and decided to have one more baby.

Life was awesome.

We had some bumps in the road, of course. Mr. Wonderful began having trouble breathing. That's a really big deal, the whole breathing thing. Especially when you're in the military and required to keep in good physical condition, a.k.a. run a lot. After several scary trips to the ER, where I was driving entirely too fast with my flashers on (sorry, Mom!), we finally got a diagnosis: severe and, at first, uncontrolled asthma. This chest tightening and constriction would happen whenever it darn well pleased, taking hold of our lives beyond just being worried that Mr. Wonderful's army career was in jeopardy.

But in the midst of the fear came joy; the stick turned blue! We would indeed be adding a new baby to the family. I would be a mama of four. I would be a mama of four! I would be a—whoa. After a teensy bit of hyperventilation, I was totally on board with our new reality. The exciting news was all we could think and talk about. I scheduled an appointment with my BFF obstetrician, and Mr. Wonderful carried on, albeit with his inhaler in tow.

Sometimes, if it happens slowly enough, you don't notice life falling apart around you. I got a phone call from Mr. Wonderful one weekend afternoon as he was driving home from our good friend Joseph's house. He and Joseph had been doing some manly work things all afternoon. I'm vague about this because I'm not sure what manly work things consist of, although I'm fairly certain it included some cussing and beer drinking. There was about seventy miles of lonely road between our homes, and Mr. Wonderful was having an asthma attack that wasn't even fazed by his inhaler. He asked me to find the nearest hospital and said that he saw a police officer and was going to try to flag him down. Then the phone went dead.

I am not usually a scaredy-cat. I'm sure if I stopped to think about all of the ugliness in this world too long, I would be a basket case, but I usually have a fairly optimistic outlook. When I lost contact with Mr. Wonderful—knowing he couldn't breathe, that his lips would be turning blue and that he might pass out at any moment—I'll admit to feeling fear. As I was frantically calling each local police dispatch near the area, I felt this awful black thing rising inside me. Trying to remain calm, I also called Joseph, who jumped in his truck and went racing off to see if he could find Mr. Wonderful as well.

Praying was all I could think to do while I kept getting put on hold as each dispatch was trying to locate their officers near him. When my phone finally rang and it was Mr. Wonderful calling from the back of an ambulance, I cannot tell you how incredibly thankful I was to hear that he was being safely transported to the hospital. Later, we were even able to laugh that our family had now seen enough drama to last us a lifetime.

We couldn't know then that the drama was just beginning.

Ironically, during this season of our lives when we had breathing on the brain, it seemed like we would just catch our breaths when that next thing would knock the wind out of us again. A few days after all the drama with Mr. Wonderful's asthma, I started the cramping. And then the bleeding. And then the losing of a baby we had prayed and longed and hoped for.

Someone said at least it was an early loss. Those are hard words to hear when you're the one doing the losing. I turned inward on my grief, throwing myself into my family, my work. Mr. Wonderful turned inward as well, and we just went on about life. We didn't talk about it much. I wanted to, but I could see Mr. Wonderful was having his own struggles. So we each struggled alone.

Around this same time, our life was getting weird. Or, I should say, weirder. It has always been a little strange at our house, but now it was getting dark. And cloudy. I could feel that the winds were picking up, and there was a big storm about to blow in. Mr. Wonderful had been really sad. Like desperately sad. So sad I found him curled up on the floor in the fetal position sobbing uncontrollably. This was completely out of his character, so I called Dennis, another one of his best friends, to help me get him an emergency appointment at the local air force base. I was frightened enough by this point to ask Dennis to take the guns from our house. Mr. Wonderful didn't want to go to the doctor despite his sadness. He told me that admitting any kind of mental-health issue was seen as a weakness and a career ender within his command. However, we got an emergency appointment scheduled at the base—three weeks later.

....

Sidebar: Our experience has been that the military doesn't know what to do with any kind of mental-health issue. At the time of our story, the two mental-health doctors at the base assigned to treat any of the possible hundreds of thousands of military personnel were just overwhelmed. Prescriptions are doled out without the near-constant supervision it requires to get dosages and medicine types right. Combine that with the "soldier-on" school of thought, add a dash of self-medication with alcohol, and you have a recipe for disaster when it comes to mental health in the military.

....

But back to our story.

Our doctor's appointment on base finally came, medicine was prescribed, and my tough army guy was told he was good to go. He tried to soldier on at work. He tried to soldier on at home as well. In the middle of all this soldiering on, we found out we were pregnant yet again. After our early loss, plus all the new chaos we were facing, I just couldn't let myself get too excited about this pregnancy.

As 2013 wore on, I barely even had time to think about it because Mr. Wonderful was beginning to come undone. At first, it was just minor unravelings. They were so miniscule that, to the naked eye, they were almost indiscernible, like a thread hanging off the bottom of a sweater. I didn't notice that he was changing until the changes were much more terrifying. I didn't realize the extent of his suffering until it was almost too late.

Then in September of 2013, life just spun out of control. Mr. Wonderful was drinking more. He forgot places and people. He started saying and doing things that were so far out of his character that I didn't recognize most of him. He became delusional and paranoid in both his speech and actions.

He couldn't read a map.

This may not sound like a big deal, but my Mr. Wonderful was an army guy who always knew where he was at any given time. When I was lost, which was somewhat frequent, I could call him up, name off one or two crazy landmarks and random street names, and he could figure out where I was. Our friends became his enemies, and total strangers became his friends. He passed out in our front yard more than once, lying facedown in vomit and grass clippings. At that point, I was too pregnant to do anything but turn his head. He was suffering so much, but there didn't seem to be anything I could do to ease his pain.

Where did the man I married go? I begged God for answers.

A few years before the undoings of our 2013, I had what I now believe was a divine appointment. I was on an elevator at a random work luncheon. A lovely lady named Debi Martin was also on the elevator, and between floors, she and I started talking. I told her I ran a foundation that gave money to nonprofits; she told me she had a nonprofit. I gave her my business card, and we stepped off the elevator.

Debi ended up applying for a grant, and I began visiting with her about her organization, The First Tee. It was a mentorship/leadership program disguised as a golf program. After The First Tee became a grantee of the Wegener Foundation, Debi and I began a relationship that would one day save my husband's life.

Obviously, I didn't know this at the time I met her, or I would've hugged her neck.

It's amazing how God works. He can put people in your life who will someday be answers to questions you haven't even thought of yet. At the time, you have no inkling how that person is going to change your life. I had no idea that when I began begging for answers, God already had one in place.

Debi and I regularly met for lunch as colleagues. We both loved to eat, and in the throes of 2013, as I was quite pregnant and in a bacon phase, I *really* loved it. One day, when I was at my wits' end and fearing for my husband's life, Debi called me up for a lunch out of the clear blue sky. For some reason on that very day, she opened up to me about her Vietnam veteran husband and what their lives looked like before he got help for his PTSD. She told me about his drinking and how scary things were at their house and how she didn't recognize the man she had married. As she was telling her story, I realized she was telling mine. I left that lunch with such gratitude. I finally had an idea of what might be going on with Mr. Wonderful.

Now I just had to figure out how to help him.

I have probably forgotten nearly everything that I learned in law school. In fact, just this week, one of my sons overheard someone ask me if I was a lawyer, to which he exclaimed, "You're a lawyer?!" Obviously, at this point, you would not want to hire me for lawyering. However, one thing that has stuck with me beyond law school is my mad researching skillz. I have to use a *z* because they're *that* good. After digging into the military system, I found out I could talk to Mr. Wonderful's commander and doctor and request a command-driven mental health evaluation. That is military jargon for, *They could force him to go to treatment.*

I asked everyone I knew to pray for that meeting with the doctor and commander. I was seven and a half months pregnant and had concerns that I would been seen as a hysterical pregnant woman, mostly because, by then, I was a hysterical pregnant woman. Armed with all the legalese I could remember and with Mr. Wonderful's doctor already in our corner, I informed the commander that his soldier was a walking liability—and that his soldier was going to kill himself or someone else if he wasn't sent to treatment ASAP.

The commander agreed to my request and asked that I give him until Monday to get Mr. Wonderful to treatment because the wheels of the military take a little time to get rolling. Since it was already Thursday, I told him we would be fine until then. I didn't know we would barely survive the weekend.

Friday, Mr. Wonderful got home from training and almost immediately proceeded to drink himself into a stupor. He left, driving drunk. I called the police. I explained to the nice officers standing on my front porch when they couldn't find him that this was all new territory. I had never called the cops on anyone before, much less my husband. Mr. Wonderful eventually came home, fell into a boozy slumber, and was still sleeping when I went to my niece's birthday party the next morning. Thankfully, the big boys were at their dad's for the weekend. I just had Little Sister, so we partied it up at Chuck E. Cheese's with my family.

When I got home, Mr. Wonderful's truck was still there. I didn't see him, so I assumed he went for a run. I put Little Sister down for her nap then tried to take one myself. I was in my third trimester—all I wanted to do was nap and eat bacon. But I just couldn't rest. Something kept nagging at me. I kept going over and over it in my mind: I saw

Mr. Wonderful's phones, his wallet, and his inhaler in the kitchen. His phones, his wallet, his inhaler. His inhaler—he never went running without his inhaler.

The moment I had that thought, a voice said, rather insistently, *Go outside.*

When you're in an empty house except for a two-year-old little girl and a voice tells you to go outside, *you go outside.* At the time, we lived on five acres surrounded by fields, with only one neighbor next to us on another five acres. That was a lot of territory for this exhausted pregnant mama. Thanks to his asthma, I hadn't gotten very far when I heard Mr. Wonderful cough from inside our kids' tree house.

Let me give you an awkwardly hilarious mental image of me in this moment: I was third trimester pregnant, and I was scaling up the ladder to the tree house like a very pregnant Spider-Man. This tree house that Mr. Wonderful had lovingly put together for our kids bit by bit in his spare time was the stuff of imaginations. It was a fort, a hideout, and spy headquarters just like the tree house that my Grandpa Stanley had built me as a kid. When I finally got to the top and my eyes adjusted to the darker inside, I saw Mr. Wonderful in the corner. He had been writing something, and there was a half-empty bottle of vodka nearby.

I still hadn't noticed that shotgun.

As I approached him, all I could feel was the sadness and sickness pouring off him so thick and awful, like all the joy in the world had been sucked out, leaving behind a giant black hole of despair. His grief left an almost rancid taste in my mouth. To this day, I have no idea what I said. Minutes or hours could have passed; I'm not sure how long we were there. All I know is I prayed like I have never prayed for God to help me get Mr. Wonderful safely out of that tree house so we could get him to treatment.

It is surely only by the grace of God and his own hand that the hugely pregnant girl somehow managed to get the drunk and suicidal soldier more than twice her size safely out of the two-story tree house and onto solid ground.

Later, after Mr. Wonderful was safely ensconced in treatment, I would read what he had been writing in his notebook that day in the tree house. There were good-bye notes to us all, even to the baby whom he had never met that I was carrying in my belly. The very last thing he had written was that he was scared, that he had done a test run, and that he could reach the trigger while the shotgun was in his mouth.

Minutes. I'm pretty sure that I was minutes from planning a military funeral and having a baby alone and figuring out how to raise four kids by myself while grieving the devastating loss of my soul mate. I know that without the people God placed in my life long before I would so desperately need them—like Debi and our couple friends, the Morrises and the Squires—I would have been writing very different words to you now as a widow.

The end of our beginning would have been the end of our story.

The special thing about endings, though, is that even with the pain of the end comes the beginning of something new. I can now see that our tree house moments—the ones that nearly took my husband and the daddy of our house—were actually the start of our realization that God wasn't finished with us yet. That he still had a plan and a destiny for our family. That he was faithful.

I am in awe at the goodness of God. As long as I live, I will bask in his grace because on that day—the day where we were so bent that we were nearly broken into a million impossibly tiny, unfixable pieces—God held us in the very palm of his hand. He softened then strengthened the bent places, lovingly melding them all back together again, bent piece by bent piece. He rejoined and enjoined us as a three-stranded chord that could not be broken, and he began a new chapter for us. That tree house was the end of our beginning. And the beginning of our story to and through PTSD.

We got horribly bent.

But in our bending came hope.

And love.

And renewal, just like God promises.

Beauty from ashes—you don't have to look any further than our family to see that this is possible. And if it is possible for us, my friends, there is hope that it is possible for you too.

....

National Suicide Prevention Lifeline
1-800-273-TALK (8255)
Veteran's Crisis Line
1-800-273-TALK (8255) Press 1
Text Message Help
838255
TTY Services for Hearing Impaired
1-800-799-4889

....

Trigger Warning

Crazy Is the New Normal

You know it's going to be one of those days when your first phone call of the morning is to Poison Control. As I caught up with the nice people there who are all good friends now since I've called before, I found out that I did not need to head to the ER to have the baby's stomach pumped for drinking Tylenol straight from the bottle.

Don't judge.

The childproof lid was on, and it was up high in a cabinet. I did all the right things, but our littlest one is Baby Houdini. He is also apparently a baby genius. I thought I would have more time. These things aren't supposed to happen until he's about three.

Visualize with me a day in the life of our family: I'm sitting quietly at my computer, working or squeezing in some writing time whenever I can. All around me, the five-ring circus is in full swing. I don't need to run away to the circus; I live in the circus. In fact, let me introduce you.

In one ring of my Traveling Circus is my former army-guy husband who suffers from PTSD, traumatic brain injury, and asthma. We call this triangle of awesomeness the *Mad Cow*. The Mad Cow makes things really interesting around our house. Not to get too sciencey, but Mr. Wonderful's brain is now different from what it used to be. This causes all kinds of fun symptoms. One of my most favorite is his short-term memory loss. Mr. Wonderful might ask, "Did we already have a conversation about this?" To which I respond, "Yes, and you totally agreed with me on everything."

Just kidding. I think it shows growth and maturity on my part that I haven't said this yet. Plus, he would totally know I was lying.

Whenever he forgets a conversation or loses a word midsentence or has what we now affectionately call a Mad Cow moment, Mr. Wonderful will start mooing. Because sometimes you just have to laugh. It helps to have a sense of humor about these things. His ringtone is a cow mooing like she's about to give birth or become hamburger. Never in my wildest dreams did I imagine that I would become a caregiver for my husband, who was younger than me. Yeah, I totally cougared that guy. I imagined that maybe someday far, far into the future, I might have to care for him. The ladies in my family live forever, so I figured it was a possibility.

I just could not have guessed that my caregiving would begin when he was thirty-five. So many doctor's appointments, red tape, paperwork, panic attacks, nightmares, therapies, medications, moments of confusion, anger, and sadness are now part of our new normal. He is getting better bit by bit, appointment after appointment, moment by moment, but it is still a long road and the biggest mountain we've ever faced.

At the core of him, though, he's still my lionhearted Mr. Wonderful, my best friend and my soul mate. It just takes a lot more effort on his part to be that man on a daily basis.

In another ring of the Traveling Circus is the death-defying daredevil Baby Houdini. He gets out of far more scrapes by the skin of his teeth than should be realistic for a one-year-old. This is the kid where I usually hear a bit of silence then loud noises, followed by a few seconds of either laughing or crying, depending on how bad his little stunt went. I often walk into Baby Houdini's mayhem after he's fallen down the stairs or climbed up the side of them, crashed into the piano bench, run into a corner of something, or jumped off a high piece of furniture and miscalculated his landing.

This is the kid that must live life to the fullest. This is also the kid I want to wear a football helmet on a daily basis. Baby Houdini is always bursting with joy and insists on going everywhere by running at full speed, even though he hasn't learned to stop quickly yet or turn sharp corners. His favorite phrase is, "Yet's go!" and he's always ready for whatever adventure he will go on with his family. He's the kid my other three put in a box with some toys, a blanket, and a water bowl. Like a dog. And they named him Reece. He was cool with it, though, laughing and playing in that box as if being his siblings' pet was the best thing ever. He also answers to Bacon, but we will get to this in another chapter.

Another circus ring is for Little Sister, our three-year-old multitalented little redheaded she-child. She can't decide if she's going to be a princess or a lion tamer or a trapeze artist, so she usually does all of them. While wearing sequins. She might be my daughter after all. She goes through life carefully planning her steps—watching her back, scanning the room, and being instantly suspicious of strangers who try to engage her. She's definitely Mr. Wonderful's daughter.

Little Sister loves her bubbas fiercely, sometimes too much so. She will take them all to task, not scared or intimidated by these boys bigger and stronger than she is. They usually end up bending to her will as she wears them down. She wears me smooth out. The adorableness and strong-willedness wrapped up in this little package is truly something to behold.

Everyone usually plays multiple roles in our Traveling Circus. When things are getting too heavy and we all just need a laugh, we have our clowns, Baby Houdini and Little Brother, the almost seven-year-old. They arrive in the middle of the show in a too-small toy car (this is when I usually hear the circus music in my head), and they work so hard to make us smile, doing silly things or making up shows within our circus. These minishows involve some sort of dancing, costume changes, loud noises, possibly a rap, and—if we had any gaseous foods—farting. I'm not sure why farting is so hilarious, but when Little Brother lets one rip and then Baby Houdini follows with perfect comedic timing by making farting sounds with his mouth, that makes for some good laughs around here.

We should charge admission.

Little Brother is also the resident ninja. He has the costume to prove it. I've lost many a beautiful knickknack and some favorite coffee mugs to his ninja skills. He finds it difficult to walk anywhere, instead choosing to catapult or cartwheel himself places. And as he believes he is an actual superhero, he is constantly trying to save the day, even if the day does not require saving.

Big Brother is our fifth grade accountant. He is also the first (only) trombonist for our Traveling Circus. He makes sure to remind me when the pantry's running low, that the kids need money for picture day or a sno-cone at school, or when it looks like he needs new shoes. He hasn't been in band yet, so as the solo trombonist, he is adding flavor and spice to our already quite noisy home. We are all very excited for him to start band this year and learn about the instrument he has already been bah-RUMP-ing all through the house.

And then there's me, a grateful, over-caffeinated mama just trying to get into this new groove: four exceptionally amazing and active kids, Mr. Wonderful and his Mad Cow, and my day job, in addition to marketing one book while writing another. Some days I feel like I'm hanging on by a fingernail.

Thank goodness for friends and family and church and babysitters. That's about the only way I have been able to sit in the middle of this storm and remain calm. We are no longer in the eye of the thing, but even the fringes of the storm are often scary, and you are still going to get pretty wet.

Mr. Wonderful tells me I've collected quite a family. I think he's right. Two of our children are adopted, and two are biological, but I forget who was born from my heart and who came from my belly. Sometimes when we're out and about, I'm reminded that we really do look sort of like the United Nations of families. I tell the kids they absolutely must be on their best behavior when we go out in public. People *will* remember us. Big Brother said he wishes we weren't so interesting sometimes.

I feel you, brother.

It's hard to be different or unusual or go against the flow of what everyone else seems to be doing around you. Sometimes it feels uncomfortable to stand out or be stared at. What I am trying to instill in our children is that family can look like anything, even a five-ring Traveling Circus. Family is more about meshing than looking alike or sharing the same blood. Family is about serving and lifting one another up, but it's also about calling one another out.

Sometimes it's beautiful. Oftentimes it's a mess.

I love that Jesus didn't mind the mess. He got right in the middle of it, not caring that he was a pot stirrer, not giving a hot hoot that he and his weird band of merry followers didn't match, with one another or anyone else. He was, and still is, a collector.

His collection is pretty odd though. He collects people: the lost, the broken, the undone, the dirty, the bent, and the hardheaded. He also collects things: broken hearts, tears, yearnings, pain, regrets, sorrows. Really unlovely stuff. This collection of his is not pretty. You certainly wouldn't find it in a museum. There doesn't seem to be any rhyme or reason to his collection except that it is the bits and pieces of lives and people that no one else seems to want.

Like I said, odd.

Jesus doesn't go for the collectables that would make him money or make him famous. He doesn't seek out the most or best or brightest. He is not interested in keeping up with the Kardashians or what's big on the runway this fall or who you know or what your net worth is. He scrapes the bottom of the barrel when he seeks because his love is for everyone, especially those who need him the most.

We are all looking for his kind of acceptance, but too often we overlook him when life is going well. I am certainly guilty of this. I get to running and gunning and things are rolling along smoothly, and I think I have life all under control. I can do this on my own. I don't need anyone looking over my shoulder or holding me back. I got this.

Except that I don't.

When crazy became the new normal, as we were ticking down toward absolute destruction, I realized I did not have this at all. I had forgotten how much I needed Jesus and that I was a precious collectable to him. Even though I was at the bottom of the barrel. Even though I was broken and bent and hardheaded and undone. My value was not in what I could do for him or what I could bring to the table. My value was in Whose I am.

Our net worth in Jesus' eyes is invaluable. Precious. Irreplaceable. That's why there's only one of you in all of time and history. Maybe you have never heard this before from anyone. Maybe you have been devalued by people or opinions or failures or addictions or relationships or bosses or downsizing. Maybe you are not where you want to be, where you thought you would be. Maybe you are in debt up to your eyeballs, or your spouse left, or you don't speak to your kids, or you lost someone or yourself along the way. Perhaps you haven't felt the joy of success for a while. Maybe it has been a long time since you looked in the mirror and liked what you saw.

That is so okay with Jesus. He will take you right now, as is, no warranty. He will take you, warped or busted into bits. He'll take your cobwebby heart or feeble body or warty soul. He'll take all the ugliness that you have stuffed down inside yourself for so long that there is no more room for anything else. This is no problem. Not for Jesus.

You only have to accept that he accepts you.

He is one crazy cat, this Jesus. He takes us all at our worst, our grossest, our bed-headed, stinky-breathed, gunky-eyed glory and loves us exactly where we are. We don't have to change for him. But he is so wonderful, perfect, glorious, and loving that we *will* change *because* of him. We won't be able to help it.

Crazy is the new normal at my house. *Mad Cow* is our love story, newly revised and rewritten. It is also Jesus' love story with us. We are a Traveling Circus, spinning around this big top. But Jesus put all of us together as a tribe, a clan, a family because he thinks we are awesome.

And most days, even in the midst of the crazy love, in the midst of the circusness that is ever present, I tend to believe him.

Sis Boom Bah

When I graduated from law school, there weren't a lot of jobs for a gypsy-hippie-cowgirl-mermaid-poet, so I settled for the second best thing at the Wegener Foundation, where we give grants to non-profits in the social services arena. I love this job. It is exactly where God knew I would need to be for this season of our lives. The other passion I have these days is living life with my aforementioned Traveling Circus and then opening the door to our crazy by writing about it.

My first book, *My Pink Champagne Life*, was all about celebrating no matter what life threw at you. I wrote it during a time where life was going pretty smoothly: Mr. Wonderful and I had a meet cute and got married, got pregnant immediately, and blended our little family happily together. I wasn't under deadlines or pressure. There were no expectations. I just wrote because I wanted to write. At first, I wasn't even writing a book. Writing just felt good, like a celebration of all that was happening in our world after a long season of hard times and obstacles and worries.

This book, though, comes from a different place. *Mad Cow* has been written because I needed to write. I have to get out the message of God's goodness, all that he has done for my family and all the miracles he has worked to bring us to this point. Sometimes therapy has been my therapy, but more often, writing is my therapy, my way to make everything that has happened to us make some sort of sense. It is my way to document how God can take an ordinary family like ours and do extraordinary things to us, with us, and for us.

Writing has led me to some discoveries over the past few years. As it turns out, I am a cheerleader. Or, I should say, I am *still* a cheerleader. I have some limited experience in this area.

At the small rural high school I graduated from, it was possible to be everything. In fact, we all had to wear lots of hats, or there wouldn't be enough people to do whatever needed doing. So football players marched in the band at halftime, and student council secretaries were on the track team, and FFA presidents were baseball captains. If you don't know what FFA is, then you didn't grow up in a rural area. Don't misread it as FAA; that's a whole other thing. The Future Farmers of America was and is a driving force behind the success of many a small-town kid.

After I blew out my knee playing basketball, I decided to take up the safer sport of cheerleading. I still wanted to go to the games and support my teams and cheer on my friends—this would be perfect! I just had to try out, and then I would be living the dream.

I was somewhat bendy, had a two-inch vertical, and hadn't done gymnastics for about five years. What could possibly go wrong?

The day of tryouts, I wasn't too nervous. I had perfected my routine, and I felt pretty confident that I could do this. When my turn came, I was ready. I ran out to the center of the gym and did a roundoff back handspring as my leading (only) gymnastic move.

The next thing I remember is both the cheerleading coach and my dad asking me if I was okay—while I was lying on the floor of the gym. In front of the entire school. Oh, did I not mention that it was open tryouts, so everyone was there?

I had two choices at that point, choices that I believe helped to define my future failings and falling downs: I could either ask for a stretcher and be carried off by my humiliation; or I could get up, finish my tryout, and find humor in the moment. Though I was still a little woozy from knocking myself out in front of the whole high school, I chose to get up and get on with it. I am thankful this was in the days before everyone had cameras on their phones. This could have broken the Internet.

Unbelievably, I made the squad. I am willing to bet that I got some sympathy points, but more than that, I think maybe my unwillingness to quit in the face of absolute humiliation and pain convinced the judges that I could cheer people on no matter what obstacles I faced. And that I would probably be doing it laughing. The next few months of being called Mary Lou Retton were totally worth it. After all, she was America's sweetheart gymnast.

I may have knocked myself out, but I was going to get to cheer on my friends and my school at every football and basketball game. From the sidelines, I was going to get to be part of the celebration of every victory and a shoulder for those times of loss.

Even now, the idea of encouraging and nourishing someone's dream or idea or heart or life just sets me on fire, sometimes to the point of burning the candle at both ends. I have found myself on the cheerleading sidelines often enough to know it's my gift, my passion, and sometimes, my curse. I have had a few cheerleading incidents where my cheerleading was not wanted or needed. Thankfully, none that knocked me out again. But even though it hurts my feelings when my realness is too much for someone, I keep putting it out there so that others can see that God can use even a mess like me. Mr. Wonderful calls me a bulldog when I get hold of something because I just won't let go.

Bulldoggedness is necessary when it comes to writing a book. Something else I've discovered during the book writing process is that it is grand to think about the idea of writing a book; it is a whole other thing to actually do it. Writing the great American novel is probably not in my future. Encouraging people with my words? Now that is something I can get excited about.

Starting is hard. Finishing is even harder. There is that in-between place where you could walk away and only look back once or twice. This is tricky because it makes quitting easy. Once you quit something, even something little, it makes it easier to quit the next thing and the next thing—until you are finally faced with the choice to quit something big, and then quitting big makes it so much easier to just keep quitting. Pretty soon, you get down the road and realize there are a string of things that you have quit, things you have left behind or walked out on that you shouldn't have.

I have quit jobs and relationships. I've quit school. I have tried to quit the gym and my cell phone contract, but they won't let me. I have quit on good ideas and things that matter. I have quit on people. And God. Every time I quit something, it just made the path to quitting the next time that much easier and shorter.

That's why finishing my first book was really a necessity for me. There were many points along the way that I thought about quitting: when my confidence was low, and I wondered who in the world I was to even be writing a book; when I didn't know if I had anything of worth to say; when I couldn't find time to write. Then I had finally written the book, and the hard part began: finding a way to get it published and then marketing it—all while our lives were falling apart and then being put back together.

Finishing that book became my benchmark for convincing myself I can do something. And along with that benchmark comes a sense of healing as I write about and remember where we have been over the last few years.

This remembering, this kind of therapeutic release in the wringing out of myself for words' sake, gives me the benefit of hindsight. A way to measure our progress through time. As difficult as the last few years have been for our family, without the writing down of things—especially those wonderful silver-lining moments I needed to get me through—I am not sure I could have kept moving forward on this path.

I still have my job at the Wegener Foundation, where I get a glimpse of God's healing for hurting people on a daily basis. This is an amazing and blessed perspective to gain from a job. But writing for me is not a job. It is a need. Even though there is no one I can talk to in HR about getting more writing time or accommodations for some quiet space to write in, I still write. I can't take a sabbatical from all the Mad Cow brings just to write our story. I sneak it in wherever I can.

What does the glamorous life of this newbie author look like? I still drive my 2003 Burb to all of my book signings, my marketing materials and extra books are shoved in my already overflowing laundry room, and my eleven-year-old is my IT guy. Two of my team members can't read or write yet, and one still needs to go through potty training. My marketing budget consists of paying friends with pizza.

My first book was written accidentally and at my own pace, as an exercise in what-ifs. I would sit at my computer, cursor blinking its reminder that I needed to be putting my thoughts on paper if there was actually going to be a book. It was just me, writing and rewriting as an act of joy at the life I found myself in after things didn't go quite the way I planned.

Now I write as a way to retrospectively look at where we were so that I can appreciate the now. As our family's self-appointed historian, I document our times of trial and times of wonder so that when we are older and when our kids are grown-ups with families of their own, they can have a history book of why our family lived the way we did. Maybe it will give them insight into those days where it did not look like we knew what we were doing (because we didn't) or when things fell apart (because they did). Maybe it will help them have compassion for parents who were just doing the best they could at the time.

The form of technology that a technophobe like myself can manage and that I have with me constantly is my phone. With four kids and a day job and a husband who needs care and a house that includes the aforementioned overflowing laundry room and all the things that a busy mama's life is filled with, I have to steal my writing moments during the in-betweens of things. The only way that I can manage to get down all the words that keep bubbling up to the top of my brain is to utilize my snippets.

So I write on my phone. There, I said it. This book is brought to you by my iPhone. Though Siri and I have a complicated relationship fraught with misunderstandings

("I'm sorry, Meredith, I didn't catch that"), my phone is how I have been getting the job done. If you see me walking around, I am probably holding my phone like I'm having a conversation with someone. I'm not. I actually hate talking on the phone, a fact that has Mr. Wonderful shaking his head in wonder since I am the oversharer of the family. I get interrupted all the time (ironically, I got interrupted twice during the typing of that sentence), so I have to get things down in a permanent manner before I completely lose the thought. I am probably just talking things out, recording them before they get lost in the jumble constantly swirling about making me call my kids each others' names or forgetting where I am supposed to be driving.

I have all these kids and responsibilities, so I am not as quick as I used to be. Before I had kids, I was one sharp cookie. I didn't use a calendar or planner or phone to remind me where I was supposed to go or what I was supposed to be doing. As a musician, I could memorize a hundred pages of piano music in no time. I could remember my passwords.

With each successive child, I find that I have less capacity to remember anything. Shoot, I go through the whole list of names including some dogs that we have had before I even get to the right kid. I used to make fun of my mom Beth for doing *this exact thing*. I now also take my sweater with me everywhere we go in the summertime because the air-conditioning is too cold for me. I am one glass of tap water, no ice, and some French phrases sprinkled in my conversation from turning into my mother.

Will the real Beth Beeby please stand up?

So much has happened over the last few years, and I feel a sense of urgency to tell the world about God's goodness to our family. We only survived because of his grace and his mercy. And maybe if people can see an imperfect Traveling Circus of a family like ours finding hope and living a life of celebration despite the crazy and chaos, they might think that God's grace and mercy are for them too.

Because they are. For everyone. Available 24 hours a day, 7 days a week, 365 days a year. All the time, day or night. No matter the circumstance. Did you mess up yesterday? No worries, God is here for you today. Did you make a mistake, cause havoc, wreck someone's car, trash someone's heart, lie, cheat, or steal? Did you mess up so bad your humans won't talk to you? God's grace and mercy are here for you too.

Take it from this former cheerleader. You can't do too bad or get too far or ruin things too much for God. Now L-E-T-S-G-O, let's go!

Between the Waves

I am a filler. I like to fill up empty spaces, people, homes, and lives with beautiful things. I want everyone to be full of joy and happiness and rainbows and unicorns.

All the time.

Problem is, when you're a filler, if you're not careful, you start expecting others to fill you just like you fill them. You will be disappointed when they don't fill you up the way you need them or want them to. It becomes easy to forget others aren't responsible for your filling.

I have forgotten before. I got so busy filling up everyone else around me and our lives and our home and our way of life that I completely left myself out. It becomes a sort of control, you know. To try to keep people filled up, even if they don't ask for it or don't think they need it. I thought they needed it, so I made myself responsible for them.

I'm learning about how to fill up my own spaces now. I put in my life, my heart, my mind, and my priorities things that God is calling me to do, speak, see, hear. Others will have to fend for themselves. I'm not responsible for filling anyone. God is. Only God can come into a person's world and, with his holy presence, seep into every cracked, worn, scarred, and torn area. Only his love and joy can become someone's all.

I can't do that for you. You can't do that for me. Even if we love each other. For a while, I went around expecting Mr. Wonderful to do this for me. And when he didn't because he was too sick and hurt and wounded himself, I grew resentful. Angry. Bitter.

Even as I type those words, they're so ugly. They're gross to look at, to say, to feel in your spirit toward another human being. When the bottom dropped out of our lives in 2013, when Mr. Wonderful's suitcase got too full and then he had to go away to empty it, I was stunned and sad. Then mad. Then resentful.

Then I was just overpowered.

Overtaken.

Over it.

When he left for treatment, I was devastated and in shock at what was happening to our family. I was simultaneously sad and relieved. My sweet and strong Mr. Wonderful was getting necessary treatment to help with sobriety, PTSD, traumatic brain injury. He was two hundred miles away in a treatment facility where military heroes like himself could learn coping skills, get medications worked out, be with other soldiers who understood him and what he had been through because they were in a similar hell.

I was back at home with three kids, trying to stay pregnant with our fourth, heartsick and in my own version of hell. I was completely overwhelmed.

Drowning.

The everyday responsibilities of getting kids to school and buying groceries and doing laundry and working at my job and being on modified bedrest, and worrying about my husband and feeling sad and traveling five hours round-trip every Saturday just to see him for an hour or two were so much. I was still reeling from the fact that the Mad Cow had tried to take my husband away from me; that when I wasn't looking, he became an alcoholic in a quest to ease his pain; that our lives had imploded inside the four walls of our home to the point that I didn't see how the pieces of us could ever be put back together.

Drowning.

Every day after Mr. Wonderful went away to treatment was just another day I had to try and survive. A day that I cried out to God to give me strength to walk through, or more realistically, for him to carry me through. Every morning I would wake up and find tears streaming down my face from my nightmares. I would actually feel the bed next to me to see if Mr. Wonderful was sleeping beside me because it had all been just a bad dream.

Every morning.

I was in such denial at first that it was like my own personal version of *Groundhog Day*. Remember that movie? Where Bill Murray wakes up and everything happens the same every day, and he can't figure out how to change it? The end of 2013 was like that for me. Wake up crying, feel the bed, realize Mr. Wonderful was indeed gone, remember what brought us to this place, cry out to God. Rinse, repeat. I couldn't wrap my head or my heart around the fact that our life was now so different.

I did not sign up for this.

This was not what Mr. Wonderful promised our life would be like. I railed against this new reality for a while because I couldn't bear the thought that Mr. Wonderful had become so sick inside that he might not return to us. At all. Or even as himself. I couldn't decide what would be worse: not having him in our lives or having a version of him that was still unrecognizable to any of us.

Even the ocean's tide recedes, giving the shoreline a break, but the drowning feeling I had just would not subside. I wasn't anywhere near the shore. I was in the eye of the storm, and as the waves tossed me to and fro, I had nothing to cling to. No one who understood. No life jacket to save me.

I have always been obsessed with the sea. I love mermaids and water. One version of my name even means "keeper of the sea." Ironically, I live in a landlocked state, but I still tell my daughter we're mermaids. I'm the mermaid queen, and she's the mermaid princess. We swim like fish, we are drawn to the water, we can't live without it.

But even a mermaid queen can be tossed about in an ocean storm if she's too close to the surface. Even a strong swimmer will have a hard time in the midst of rough seas. Drowning is possible. Being pulled under, probable.

During the stormy waters, I cried out to the only one who could save me. I called on the same Jesus who told Peter to walk upon the water. Though I had fallen in and my faith was weak, he was there to pull me into the boat.

The ride was still rough, but between the waves was where I was finally able to catch my breath, batten down the hatches for the next wave, and take a moment to regroup. The waves of any storm come fast and furious, not caring that you can't seem to find your sea legs or that you're nauseous or that you can't even find a spot to hunker down in. They just come. They wash over you, again and again, battering you with an almost incomprehensible force. But if you're hanging on to Jesus as tightly as I was, you feel a sense of awe that he is keeping you from being swept overboard.

Between the waves was where I started to see that our life, though not what I thought it would be and not what I had hoped for, was still a place of joy. Every day that I managed to keep our precious baby inside my belly—the baby whom I now wanted and needed more than ever—was a good day. Every week that I could add on to my sweet munchkin's baking time in my ever-growing oven was a victory not to be taken for granted.

And each week that I got to visit Mr. Wonderful in the hospital and see some of the progress he was making there, knowing he was working so hard to come back to our splintered family, was a treasure. He would proudly tell me of all the things he had been working on, his medicine changes, what his doctors said. And I would tell him about the funny things the kids did or how my doctor's appointments went. I brought him ultrasound pictures and cards from the kids. We started a brand-new marriage in that hospital; our old one died in the tree house where I found Mr. Wonderful on that awful day. The hospital that was helping Mr. Wonderful heal was the place where it seemed we got married all over again, getting to know each other like it was the beginning of our relationship.

The waves of pain and heartache still washed over me and, at times, threatened to wash me completely away. But between the waves, when I would try to catch my breath, Jesus was calming the storm, sending me everything I needed during that time.

My parents dropped everything they had going on and, at least twice a week, came to my house, helped with laundry, bought us groceries. They made me put my feet up like the doctor said and forced me to relax. My mom and dad paid attention to my three kids, who couldn't quite figure out what was going on with Daddy gone and Mama so sad and stressed. They made me laugh, pampered me, reminded me I wasn't alone, took care of our kids, and reassured me that God put Mr. Wonderful in that hospital to keep him safe and help him heal so I didn't have to worry about him.

And our friends—oh, our friends! They mowed our *five acres* of land. They threw me a baby shower not because I really needed anything but because they wanted to cheer me up. They came over and kept me company and changed air filters and lightbulbs so I wouldn't stand on a ladder. They rearranged rooms and put together baby furniture so I wouldn't do it on my own.

During that time, Mr. Wonderful did everything he could to show me he was working to come home to us. He tried, even through the hard days, to show us love. To pray with me. To tell me how much he missed me and the kids. To tell me he was proud of me. Though we didn't get to talk every day—and when we did, it was usually just for a few minutes—he tried to convey in those short conversations that he was still *all in*.

At times, I thought there was a fair to middlin' chance that I wouldn't survive the heartache, the missing my husband, the worry, the stress, the pregnancy, the unknown. My Jesus sent friends and family to care for me, ensuring my survival so that Mr. Wonderful would have a home, a family, and a wife to come home to.

Between the waves is where I experienced the greatest amount of God's grace and love that I have ever known. The pauses between when one wave would crash into me and the next would continue the job of knocking me over—the place where I was truly the most vulnerable—was where I felt God's love pouring out, spilling over, filling me up.

It's where I realized I didn't have to be the filler anymore. Where I figured out how much I was loved by my Creator, the one who made each star and universe but still cared about every detail of my sad and battered world. Where I felt great peace despite the circumstances, despite the hurt, despite the waves.

I realized I didn't even need to fill my own spaces. All I had to do was open my eyes, open my heart, and accept the beauty, the love, and the new mercies God had waiting for me every day. He called me out upon the waters; and though my feet failed, when I called on his name, he saved me.

He saved us. And if you happen to be between the waves right now, he will save you too.

Bacon

Let me give you a little backstory.

For over two decades, I was a quasi-vegetarian. I didn't have any problem with anyone eating meat—I just didn't want to, which was ironic as my Grandpa Clyde was a farmer who also raised cattle. My family didn't understand my whole meat-is-gross stance. As a little kid, I had the nightly war of the wills with my mom, the standoff always over eating anything resembling meat. These only ended when either 1) she finally took pity on me, or 2) it was bedtime.

Oh, how I prayed for a dog.

My grandma never could wrap her mind around the fact that I didn't eat meat. Even when I was a grown-up who hadn't eaten meat in years, nearly every time I went to her house, she offered me chicken fried steak. And when I would remind her that I didn't eat meat, she would ask if I would rather just have a quick ham sandwich. Complete denial.

When Mr. Wonderful and I first began dating, he was understandably dismayed when he found out I wouldn't be trying his famous rack of lamb. The classic hunter-gatherer who actually hunted some of the meat he ate somehow ended up dating a (mostly) vegetarian. It is nothing short of a miracle that we made it through that conversation.

Fast-forward to the beginning months of 2013. I was hungry. And I was angry—like, wanting to throat-punch people angry. This was so not me. After a couple of weeks of this, it dawned on me that I might be pregnant. I was afraid to hope, though. We had wanted to add to our family for a while, but we had already gotten a positive pregnancy test. And then, for whatever reason, the pregnancy ended.

That's a hard moment, when you realize that you're not pregnant anymore. That kind of loss breaks off pieces of your heart, changes you from the inside. For me, that loss made me feel fear when I took another pregnancy test. And another and another and another until I had an entire collection of tests confirming the presence of a baby that I was praying would stick this time.

After our loss, Mr. Wonderful and I had talked about waiting to have any more babies. He had been experiencing health issues: first, asthma, then something else we couldn't put our finger on. The timing of this pregnancy was laughable to me. Between my fear that I would lose this baby too, and the changes I was slowly seeing in Mr. Wonderful, I didn't enjoy the pregnancy like I should have.

My man-sized appetite and desire to engage in physical violence convinced me we were having a man-child. I loved being a boy mom, so I was trying to be cautiously optimistic. Something else unusual started happening: I wanted to eat *bacon*. Me, the girl who wouldn't touch the stuff even when I was a little bitty thing. Now I only craved bacon. I needed bacon. It was all I could think about, getting my hands on some bacon. I figured it was a passing fancy, but it turned out nothing else would do. Not turkey bacon. Not "facon." It had to be the real deal; and the crispier, the better.

I'm sure my triglycerides went through the roof during my pregnancy. I was eating bacon like I had to make up for all the decades of lost time. No one around me could believe it—this baby was making me eat bacon! Mr. Wonderful was so happy. He didn't even question it; he just began cooking other meaty specialties to see if my pregnancy taste buds would fall for it. I ate more red meat during 2013 than I had my entire life all put together.

And it was awesome.

We started calling the baby Bacon. We didn't realize at the time we would eventually be forced to change his name to Baby Houdini—his escape skills weren't evident in utero. Who was this little creature in my belly moving with such force that I craved meat? I began to let myself think about what a gift this baby would be even though, currently, our life was getting turned upside down. As Mr. Wonderful began acting erratic, I began having early contractions at twenty-seven weeks, so I was put on medicine and modified bed rest.

Riiiiiiight. Bed rest for a working mom with three other kids.

After everything came undone in that tree house, life moved so fast to get Mr. Wonderful to treatment that we didn't have a chance to talk about how we would explain his absence. I wasn't sure what he would be comfortable with me discussing, so I told all but our closest friends that he was at a military training, which was true in a way. For the first time in his adult life, he was learning how to cope without using alcohol, and he was getting the beginnings of a lifelong education about PTSD and traumatic brain injury. We both were. We were starting to understand how the Mad Cow could show up years after the deployment, especially in the soldier-on environment of the military.

As bad as things got, once Mr. Wonderful went to the hospital for treatment, I felt a sense of relief even through my heartbreak. Even though I was seven and a half months pregnant, even though I was supposed to be on bed rest while making sure three other kids were fed, clothed, and wherever they were supposed to be, I felt peace. I knew Mr. Wonderful—after months of me and my pregnant belly scurrying around trying to save him from certain death—was finally in a safe place. After watching him suffer horribly, it was a weight off my shoulders to know that he was getting the help he needed. And though we had no idea what the road ahead would be like, I felt Jesus pressing into my heart that this time of separation for us was going to be a blessing. I just didn't believe him at first.

Our life then wasn't pretty. Mr. Wonderful was in a lockdown mental hospital for military heroes with PTSD and substance-abuse problems one state over. To be clear, it was the kind of place where they take your shoelaces. Where someone would watch him shave each morning. Where while there were visiting hours on Saturdays, we had to be monitored during visitation, and I had to leave my cellphone in the car. This new world we entered was a shock to both of us. There would be no end in sight for the foreseeable future. His original placement in treatment for twenty-eight days was extended because of all the pain and trauma that the Mad Cow had already wrought on his body, mind, and soul. His release would depend on his various diagnoses, treatment plan, and how well he responded. I learned that some of the soldiers there had been in the hospital for many months.

That two-hundred-mile one-way drive gave me time to think about our life, which wasn't always a good thing. All alone in my car was when I could let my guard down and cry out to God. I sobbed the big ugly cry of grief that one feels when you lose someone. In the beginning, I was sure that I had lost the Mr. Wonderful I had known. I was certain that I would be raising our babies by myself because I could not fathom how a man as wounded as he was could ever be put back together to return to us.

The kids came with me only once. I knew it would lift his spirits, but I also didn't want them to see him in that place. I didn't want them to have memories of the big strong daddy of our house so busted up. Besides, I knew that having visitors—even his biggest fans—was mentally and emotionally exhausting for him. In the beginning of what became a two-month stay, I was in denial that this was our new life. I didn't realize that I would be the caregiver for my husband. I had no idea where my capable, confident man had gone. Would he ever return? Would I recognize the guy who would leave treatment and come home with me? Would our marriage, our family, and our children survive all of this?

Would I?

These were the questions I asked God. I yelled to God. I begged God to answer. As my due date approached, I began to face the possibility that Mr. Wonderful might not even be at the birth of his son. I somehow had to prepare myself that I might have to give birth to our baby alone, that I might have to raise kids with him present physically but unable to participate in our lives. Each Saturday that I would visit, I could see flashes of the guy whom I had fallen in love with, but I wondered how fast he could make progress. I worried that his progress might not continue in the stress of our real, messy everyday life.

Only by God's hand and the mountain of prayers that my friends and family covered us with did that baby stay safely in my belly until my scheduled C-section at thirty-nine weeks. The day before our son was born, I anxiously waited to pick up Mr. Wonderful at the air force base. He would be released into my care for one week so that he wouldn't have to miss the birth of our son. This reunion between us was a moment that still brings me tears and a smile. We were both so nervous and excited to see each other again—we were like two teenagers reunited at summer camp. As we hugged and cried and thanked God for bringing us back together, I felt so blessed that we had made it to this point. Mr. Wonderful was going to be with me for the birth, a memory I had feared he would miss. Though he would have to return to the hospital to finish out his treatment, we would have him home for that first precious week of our baby boy's life.

That Friday of Bacon's birth was intense. I was so anxious: what if Mr. Wonderful freaked out or his PTSD got triggered? What if I freaked out? We were both brand-new at the types of coping skills we needed to handle the Mad Cow triggers. And now our new skills were going to be put to a real-world test: the birth of a baby. That's enough life change for anyone to lose it over, but this was unknown territory for us.

I was wheeled into the operating room to get prepped for surgery, leaving Mr. Wonderful by himself. As they were numbing me, I prayed that we would get through this, that our precious baby boy would be okay, and that Mr. Wonderful would be okay too. When it was time for him to come in and hold my hand, we had a tender moment that has been burned into my heart. He said a prayer for us and kept reassuring me that everything was going to be all right. As I was crying my way through the surgery, Mr.

Wonderful never took his eyes off me. He kept touching my face and wiping my tears and telling me everything was going to be okay. This steady man, this rock, this guy holding my hand was again the man I had known before our world came crashing down.

As our newest baby was born, something else was born right alongside Bacon in that moment too: a brand-new us with a brand-new normal. Our life together was no longer going to be like the life we had. Our expectations of ourselves and each other were going to have to change fairly drastically so that we could form this new family. As we were in the operating room and Bacon (a.k.a. Baby Houdini) was placed beside me, I knew that this path was not going to be the easy road. We were in for some hard times. But now I knew that we were in this new normal together, and for the first time in more than a year, I breathed a sigh of relief.

This little baby, this Bacon, was such a joyful blessing during a very hard time. He was one of the ways God saved us in his perfect timing. If my other pregnancy had gone full term, that baby would have been born in the middle of the mess instead of during Mr. Wonderful's lifesaving treatment. God's plan for us was that this eight-pound bundle of joy would be a healing ointment for our family. That's a lot of pressure on a kid, I know. But instead of being a stressor or a Mad Cow trigger like I feared, Bacon became the catalyst for our new life lived with gratitude. When you walk to the edge of death, daily living takes on a whole different perspective. I couldn't help but be overflowing with joy at this new life.

Even though I would have no sleep, even though Mr. Wonderful had to return to treatment and life as we knew it was no longer, even though our finances were in shambles and Mr. Wonderful's army career was probably over—all of that faded into the background once our Bacon was born. Because he was God's promise to me from back when I was pregnant and alone and hurting and sad and desperate and on my knees: I wasn't truly alone, and there was still joy to come in the morning.

My every tear, my every hurt and cry and broken piece was gently tucked away when my sweet boy was born because God answers prayers—in big, miraculous, glory-filled ways. I believe he did this for us so I would be able to tell everyone about how close we came to death and destruction and how God saved us. I believe that he wants people to hear our story so that if they happen to be in a place of darkness or pain or suffering, they will see his light shine through our brokenness as a beacon of hope.

Miracles still happen. My family is living proof of that. Mr. Wonderful is alive and well. God saved our Bacon in more than one way. Our other three kids are happy and healthy and thriving. I still get to be Mr. Wonderful's wife and a mom of four.

And I still eat red meat. Will miracles never cease?

Radioactive

I'm currently feeling pretty stretched. And not in the "I just did yoga so I feel like jelly" way, more in the "I can't believe I got up early and so did one of my kids" way. I woke extra early today to have some time with Jesus, drink some coffee, and write. So of course, Big Brother got up early to annoy the schniz out of me while I am trying to write.

....

Sidebar: Schniz *is just a made-up word that was probably cool in 2005. I use it as a replacement for my driving words because I'm trying to cut back. Please don't ask me to go cold turkey.*

....

I'm a little cranky about this as I love my sleep. If I am going to interrupt my sleep time to write, please don't interrupt my writing time to annoy.

As you can see, I'm not appropriately caffeinated yet.

I probably shouldn't be writing at all yet, except I know that the wee morning hours make me a little less likely to censor myself—and you may get some good truths from me, or you may get sheer crankiness. It's a toss-up with no guarantees.

One truth I can tell you for sure is that for the last few years, it has felt like we were the family who went into a belowground bunker during a 1950s nuclear-war threat and came out in the present day. So much has changed! I have told family and friends how sorry I am that we have not been able to be there for them. Most days, for a while, we were doing only necessary things, like surviving and feeding and clothing children, so we just didn't have much room in our bunker for anything else. We don't have these days as often anymore, so I am trying to make up for the last couple of years.

When it came to friendships over these last years, I have been a taker. I freely admit that I was in such dire need of help that I took every bit offered to me; I'm not proud. I was in a time of distress, and I had friends and family who showed up and shored me up. They held my hand and, at times, held me together, without expecting anything in return.

And now that we are past the emergency, past the just surviving minute by minute as a family, I have so much to pay back. Or forward. Or however I need to do it. I have taken it upon myself to try to be a better friend. You know, the kind of friend you can count on to do crazy things with or listen or bring you coffee or groceries. The kind of friend who would wear a matching Pink Ladies jacket with you in our little gang if you asked. The gal pal who will meet you for lunch, pick up the tab, or pick up your kids. Whatever you need, that's the kind of friend I am trying to be.

I don't always do this well, though. It's not an issue with our friendship. I am always up for Pink Lady jackets or something stupid or crazy when it comes to my girlfriends. It is a definite possibility that I am leading the way on the stupid or crazy. There just seems to be an issue with my time. I am beginning to realize that I am a bit stingy with it.

Time didn't used to be so elusive to me. Or so valuable. The realization that I have squandered entire lifetimes of it over the years just makes me gag. I suppose I have never really had a grasp on time. I have always been running slightly behind the curve. Actually, because I don't run, I am often bringing up the rear, eating the dust of time despite my speed walking.

Anyone remember the show *Friends*? Who am I kidding? Of course, you do, unless you were living in a bunker too during the entire time it was on, which, I concede is entirely possible in light of the last few years we have experienced. Phoebe on *Friends* was my favorite character, quirky and strange and viewing the world through lenses that were different from anyone else's. We had lots of things in common, but the main one was our running style. If you don't remember the episode I am talking about, search it on the Internet so you will know what I look like when I run, which is why I don't. Ever. In fact, never mind.

My maiden name was Beeby, and in my family, we have a thing called the *Beeby speed*. Sounds like a good thing, right? Nope. If you're cursed with the Beeby speed, it just means that you run like Phoebe and you are slower than a slug. Unfortunately for my sweet young daughter, darling Little Sister, I have seen you run, and the Beeby speed continues in the next generation! You will probably need to stick to sports that don't require speed, like curling or table tennis. Why do you think we moved to a larger school district? The education? Nope. It's for choices in sports so you won't humiliate yourself the way I did for years.

I speed-walk through life, but my grasp of time still gets further and further away. I just want to bend it into a protective circle around my life instead of feeling like I am chasing it. With so many demands that I cannot figure a way around, I often feel stuck. And stingy. And downright miserly.

I seem to swing from one extreme to the other. I went from needing my friends so desperately to now wanting to repay their kindnesses by saying yes to everything. This is not healthy either. I want to be such a good friend, to be counted on, to take time when it is needed, and put everything else to the side so that I can hold your new baby or cry with you because your husband left, or go the extra mile to be at your event, or sit with you when you're sick, or bring you something to cheer you up when you're feeling down.

I want to be all these things to all of my people, but I just can't. I love you, dear friends; and if crazy weren't the new normal at my house, I would be everywhere you wanted me to be. But right now, you may have to settle for a text message that says I'm praying for you, and I actually will be. Or that I can meet for coffee for just a sec. Or that I heard you weren't feeling well, so I'm dropping off a meal, but I can't stay. Oh, you have coffee? Well, maybe I can stay for two minutes.

This place in my life won't last forever, I know. We are starting to come out into the light after all our time belowground. That bunker was pretty dark, and it's disconcerting how bright it is out here. My family is still trying to get our bearings in this bright place.

Part of me misses the bunker. After the atom bomb blew life as we knew it to bits, we hunkered down. Some of the radiation may have clung to our clothes and made us sick for a time, but we managed to hole up as a family. We had food and water and shelter, and we even entertained ourselves at the same time we were driving one another crazy. Now that we are aboveground again, we aren't quite sure how to behave with the Mad Cow, where to go, what to do, how to be. There still seems to be a layer of radioactive waste all around too—on our clothes, our bodies, our friendships. We are doing our best most days, and our children are much better at adapting to anything than we are. Even as the leaper of the family, I am a little thrown off by the amount of different I'm experiencing out here.

It is so good to be among the living. And as the leaper, part of me wants us to dive right in, taking our spot in life back. You can't really go back, though. You can only move forward, which we are trying to do with generosity of spirit and good humor and grace, a whole truckload of grace. Wow, that's hard.

Generosity is tough with friends and family. It gets hard to show it beyond the interaction of social media. Facebook comments, sure. That type of generosity is easy peasy. Drop by your house to bring you chicken soup—hmmm (glancing at watch). The type of generosity I am talking about is the kind that requires time, that most precious commodity. If it could be bottled and sold, I'm sure most of us would pay top dollar to have some extra on hand. I know I would.

Life can change in the time it takes to go from one beat of your heart to the next. The only guarantee each of us has is that we are dying. Probably not today. Hopefully not tomorrow. I pray not for many decades to come, but it sort of puts a damper on squandering the time we are given and makes me wish I could hoard time the way I hoard shoes. If you have ever been witness to or the recipient of a miracle, time takes on a different meaning. Time gets a new value: priceless. To look at death, to experience loss, to stare down the barrel—literally in our case—gives time a sort of preciousness it may not have held before. All of the time I have frittered away is gone forever, time I should have spent telling my loved ones how much I love and appreciate them, time I should have spent just being with my people, my tribe.

I recently heard a story about a man in our church family who had a freak accident in his pool. He was underwater for approximately six to eight minutes, was pulled out by his two sons ages eight and ten, and for all intents and purposes, died. He said something that I can't get out of my head. He said that after being dead and experiencing a miracle, it's really hard to have a bad day.

Time isn't of the essence until it is. Time is more valuable to the dying, and aren't we all doing exactly that?

As a couple, Mr. Wonderful and I have seen death. Death got so close we stared into its evil red eyes and felt its foul-smelling breath on our faces. Only by the grace of God did we walk away from it. Mr. Wonderful is a miracle. Bacon, a.k.a. Baby Houdini, is a miracle. Because of the miracles that we have experienced, even our rough days with the Mad Cow are good because we appreciate where we have been and where we could be. In that tree house, time stopped when we were at the crossroads of life and death.

That space between heartbeats could have changed everything.

As we climb out of our bunker, eyes rapidly blinking to let them adjust to natural light again and moving our muscles in ways we haven't for a while, when we have hard times or times when we're just so worn from the effort expended, it is still a good day. Every day we wake up and we are breathing is another day we get to store away as a day well lived. Another day saved as precious memories. Every day is such a gift now because we almost didn't get to have more everydays.

To our friends and family, we thank you for your patience. We thank you for your friendship. We thank you for your love and kindness and support and prayers. We don't want to be the friends we once were to you; we want to be better. We hope to be not squanderers of time but givers of ourselves, generously giving to you what you have given to us. And the further we get from that crossroads of life and death, where the space between heartbeats could have changed our entire trajectory, the better we will be at living and loving again. I am sure of it.

I am grateful for our chance at a second chance. Those of us in the small club who have had a rather dramatic life-and-death do-over through some modern-day miracle view life differently. We look through lenses colored with gratitude and humility and grace because we have been brought to what appeared to be the end, but instead of an ending before our life's work was finished, we got a new beginning. To begin again when you believe you're finished is some kind of paradigm shifter. Some kind of game changer. Some kind of divine divergence in the road.

As we emerge from our bunker and start walking through this life again, we gladly take the detour.

The Casita

I've decide that potty training a fiery redheaded she-child is kind of like training a wild tiger to dance to show tunes. It's a delicate yet frightening process that requires infinite patience, a death wish, and multiple costume changes. It's giving up nights and weekends and running the gauntlet between pull-ups and panties, big girl and baby. I mistakenly thought that potty training a girl would be easier than my boys.

It was not. I didn't take into account the fact that my daughter thinks she's a grown-up and that I was potty training her in the middle of a move with three other kids.

The reality of four children for our family is that quality control goes right out the window. Mr. Wonderful and I were barely hanging on to our zone defense with three. Now that there are four plus the Mad Cow, it's truly just survival mode. Anyone can get voted off the island at any given time. Does anyone else text their husband from inside their house just to finish a sentence? No? Uh, me either.

With the limited capacity I have for keeping an eye on all my kids at the exact same time, I have to be selective in where my watchful eye is trained. Having had a succession of three-year-olds in my home, I now know that I will get the most bang for my buck if I keep an eye on whoever is currently nearest three years old.

You'll see how I arrived at this theory in a minute.

First, let me talk to you about the process of selling a home. Did you know that when you decide to put your house on the market, you're expected to keep it constantly clean? And that you should simultaneously also be packing all of your belongings, even with four kids undoing the cleanliness and unpacking everything you may have managed to pack? I now know that moving with four children in tow makes you question your very sanity. Who does this sort of thing? People being held at gunpoint? Brave people? Stupid people? Don't answer that.

In our case, it was a mama at the end of her rope from stepping on kids everywhere she went and a daddy who wanted to keep the mama happy. Smart man. Not too long after Mr. Wonderful got home from treatment, we decided that even though it was going to be a crash course in insanity, we were going to trade some of our land for more bedrooms. We were going for it.

We should've known it wasn't going to be easy.

The day before we signed the contract to put our house on the market was just like any other day. Mr. Wonderful and I were both home. The baby was sleeping, the Bigs were playing outside, and Little Sister was happy to take a nap herself.

That should have been my first clue.

During the Littles' nap time, I was able to get so much work done. Wegener Foundation business was in order.

We packed some boxes, did some laundry. Then we went to wake up the Littles so we could all go outside together before dinner.

When I opened the door to Little Sister's bedroom, I was hit, full force and effect, in the face with—well, I wasn't sure what at first. It was like my eyeballs had been tie-dyed or a rainbow vomited. My brain couldn't take it all in. What was I even seeing? After a full ten seconds of staring, understanding was dawning on me. My almost-three-year-old daughter was covered from head to toe in what appeared to be paint. Her room was covered as high as she could reach with washes of every color imaginable. It was on her bed, the walls, the woodwork, and (choking!) the carpet.

I immediately gave myself a time-out.

Apparently, unbeknownst to any grown-up in the house, Little Sister had found five (FIVE!) tubes of finger paint and emptied them all in her room. That was in our house that we were putting on the market.

Mr. Wonderful leapt into action and immediately raced away to rent a carpet cleaner. After my lengthy time-out, I—still in shock—put Little Sister in the tub and began contemplating arson. Upon Mr. Wonderful's return, we discovered a fact that probably saved our house from a fiery end: it was washable finger paint! Praise Jesus, this just might work after all!

We were unbelievably able to get every stitch of color out of everything, and we put our house on the market without a hitch. And by without a hitch, I mean we still had the impossible job of trying to keep a house with four children absolutely spotless when it is a well-established fact in many circles that I am no domestic goddess. Without a hitch also meant we agreed to a thirty-minute lead time for house showings despite our best time of thirty-seven minutes to get four kids out of the house and buckled into all three car seats we required.

Calculate that, Common Core math.

Our amazing realtors and friends, Tara and Peter Levinson, sold our house in record time. And then, because not only are they amazing realtors but awesome people, they offered us a place to stay on their property since our new house wouldn't be ready until nine days after we moved out of our old house. God has really blessed us in the friends department. We figured we could do anything for nine days, so we happily took them up on their offer. We quickly named the little artist cottage where we would be staying the Casita. You know what *casita* means? "Little house." Keep this in mind. This was an adorable little space that, if mine, would have been my grown-up playhouse. I would only leave it when my food or art supplies ran out. If the Casita were mine, my children would constantly have to come find me when they got hungry, or it was time for bed because being artsy in it would surely make me lose track of time. It was darling! Also important to note that *darling* is real estate speak for 150 square feet of not entirely useable space.

Anything for nine days.

The bathroom was so narrow that my giant Mr. Wonderful could not enter. He is 6'6", 330 pounds, and built like he played for the NFL. His shoulders were so wide that the few times he attempted to go in, he had to turn sideways and think small-people thoughts. I'm not even exaggerating. And of course, we were potty training the aforementioned fiery redheaded she-child. With one bathroom. We immediately made the rule that if you had boy parts, you had to pee outside so as to free up the bathroom for the potty trainee. The boys were ecstatic. We get to pee outside! Mark our territory! Write our names in the dirt!

Sorry, Levinsons.

At night, the three older kids would climb up a ladder to the teeny loft when it was bedtime. A ladder! This ladder was small enough that mama had to do all the tucking in since, once again, Mr. Wonderful's ginormousness got in the way. His Hulk-esque shoulders wouldn't fit through the narrow opening of the ladder stairway either. Mr. Wonderful and I slept on the foldout couch, and the four-month-old was tucked safely under a table on a pallet. He's lucky he didn't end up in a moving box for a bed.

To orchestrate our nightly ritual, the kids would all use the restroom (outdoors and indoors) before going to bed. Once we pulled out the foldout couch, they would have to *climb over us* to get to the bathroom. Marinate on that visual for a moment.

Nine days. We can do anything for nine days.

To combat the cramped and the crazy, we immediately joined the gym and spent copious amounts of time working out. It was the healthiest we've been in forever. Mr. Wonderful was able to shower there, and we were able to take advantage of the free two-hour childcare so we could work out then talk to each other, hear other noise besides the barrage of kid noise that rattled all 150 square feet of the Casita. There were other luxuries at the gym we took advantage of as well. We used the restroom whenever we felt like it. We walked more than three feet in any direction before running into anything. We sat in chairs.

This time in the Casita made us realize that it really is the little things that matter. At nine days, we found out that our cozy living situation would last a skosh longer. Two weeks tops. So we carried on. My job got exceptionally crazy, which meant since I worked from home, my office was now in the Casita, where I couldn't find anything. And because the kids were still in their last month of school before summer break and we didn't want them to have to start a new school until fall, we drove through rush-hour traffic an hour in the morning and again in the afternoon. It was pure madness!

But as we survived the stress of packing, moving, money, potty training and working from my temporary chaotic office, we started appreciating the finer points of our situation. The kids were having the time of their lives. Every once in a while even now, someone starts talking about how much fun the Casita was. They have even asked when we can go back, as if it was a fancy vacation spot or resort that we could return to.

Our time at the Casita enriched and blessed us. We grew closer as a family because there is no other sane way for six people (seven if Mr. Wonderful counts as two) to exist in 150 square feet. We laughed so much during that time. We worked out and grabbed pizza on the way home. I said we were healthier, not perfect. We put Little Sister on the "potty train," as one of her brothers said, and she (mostly) stayed. It was a crazy, wonderful, fun, tiring, stressful, happy close-quartered blessed time that made us appreciate God's new mercies every day.

It was uncomfortable and at times untenable. But we had one another, and we had our blessed Savior. And that was truly all we needed, no matter how everything else worked out. Whether or not our new house would ever be finished, which was questionable at one point. Whether or not the fiery redhead would ever be potty trained, which was also questionable. Whether she would survive the potty train, or I would, both of which were *very* questionable. When we pulled together as a family in that glorious small confined space, we discovered how much we drove one another crazy and how much we loved one another. It was a lot on both fronts.

We watched sunshine stream in our windows to wake us as birds sang morning songs. The kids played outside because there was nothing else for them to do and nowhere to do it. Mr. Wonderful and I watched Netflix late into the night on my laptop. We snuggled and cooked creatively in the miniature kitchen. We went to church and celebrated that we were indeed blessed.

The Casita made us appreciate so much about our lives and one another. Not a night goes by that one of the kids doesn't thank God for the nice (bigger) roof over our heads now. And when they complain of nothing to do, we remind them of the Casita. And then, of course, they beg us to pee outside.

I'm pretty sure our new homeowners' association would frown on this.

God used that crazy, weird time to bless the socks off our family and to show us that his way is the only way we ever want to do things again.

Battle Buddies

Pressing In

By your forties, you really figure out who your friends are. Candlelight, yes. Fluorescents, not so much. Knit fabric? No, thank you. People who knew you when, stuck with you, have seen your ugly hairy life warts and still hang out with you? These are the ones. These are the keepers.

My friend Amy is one of these people. She and I met in law school, and though I wish I had the brilliant legal mind she did, I was a bit of a fish out of water. As preparation for the rigors of law school, I had gotten a music degree and then become a music minister. Feel free to insert sarcasm here. If a judge wanted me to sing a little ditty ('bout Jack and Diane), I would've been the girl. My basic understanding of courtroom etiquette is that they kind of frown on that. And come on, you were already hearing that song in your head. I just helped you along.

Amy gets me. Whereas I call her my little homunculus, I'm average height, which makes me a giant in her world. Whereas she's logical and analytical, I'm artsy fartsy. Whereas she knew her contracts law inside and out, you do not want me writing a contract for you. It will have loopholes that I won't know about. Let's just say contracts was not my best subject.

Most of law school wasn't my best subject.

Let me set the scene for you. Several of us would be gathered around a table arguing whatever cases had been assigned for reading that day. I would be nodding my head and making mental notes so later I could look up all the words I didn't understand. Since this was prekids, I could actually make mental notes and they would stick. Not so much now.

Did you know you have to learn a foreign language just to get through law school? Me either! I knew nothing of Latin, so I was up a creek without a paddle, as they say in these parts. Those three years of law school were the longest stretch of time where I was quiet. Mr. Wonderful would not have recognized me. I was just trying to stay under the radar, survive, and hopefully, graduate.

I was legally blonde.

Amy and I met in our legal research and writing class, the only class in law school where I felt comfortable. We started talking, and I found out that she was doing the law-school thing with two kids in tow. I was childless when I began (only a vague memory for me now), so I could not imagine how she was going to do everything law school required of us, much less raise kids.

We decided that we would make fantastic moot court partners, not to be confused with moo court, which is where Mad Cow hearings are held. Just kidding, I made that up. I decided that I would ride on her coattails to greatness, so we signed up and began preparing.

What we didn't know at the time is that we were both idiots. Why take on a whole other massive extracurricular activity that we would not even receive a grade for, one that required tons of preparation and time, when we were just trying to survive as one Ls our first semester? Looking back, I can see now it was an act of lunacy. I blame lack of sleep on that decision.

The preparation was intense and arduous, especially when added to our other reading and assignments and trying to stay on each individual professor's good side. We spent late nights at IHOP, the law school, Amy's house. We argued and practiced and researched and argued some more. We even catnapped at the law school. She still teases me to this day about my dog-haired blanket I kept at the school.

Our work together was the beginning of a friendship that has now seen nearly a decade and a half. I adopted Big Brother while in law school, and Amy was first in line to congratulate me and give me good parenting advice. We graduated with honors and went our separate work ways: she ended up being an administrative law judge, and I run a nonprofit.

But we have never stopped supporting each other. We have the kind of friendship that no matter how long it's been since we last talked—an hour, a week, a month—we just pick up where we left off. We have had those moments where one of us called, and the other dropped everything to bring comfort or aid or pray. We have seen each other through many, so many children (we now have ten together—she has two biological kids and is about to adopt her fourth child from China), and we share our stories of child-rearing with love, laughter, and more than a pound of frustration.

Little Sister—the one with the knowing looks and little old-woman wisdom—is a clinger. By this, I mean that at drop-off to mom's day out, she becomes an octopus with all of her appendages, ssschlooping on to my leg as I'm trying to walk out the door. I can almost hear the sucking sounds of her little tentacles as they latch on to me with an incredible strength one would not necessarily attribute to a three-year-old. If I take a step, her whole body comes with me. For some reason, she does not want me to leave, even though it's only twice a week for five hours. She just presses into me, trying to meld her body to mine as if I will absorb her and take her with me.

I so get this.

The last few years of our lives, I've felt like Little Sister. I've been a clinger. In the midst of my worry and sorrow and struggle, it sometimes felt like God was slipping away from me. Like he was leaving me in an unknown place with strangers who were going to make me do God only knows what kind of activities. I wasn't sure if he was coming back. I wasn't certain he would pick me up. There I was, just hanging on to his leg, begging him not to leave, crying for him to take me with him.

Of course, he never really left.

I see that now. He let me cling when I needed to and let go when I finally felt ready and steady enough to. Not to do things on my own, of course, but to use the strengths and courage that he had given me to cope with whatever I was facing in the moment. All the while, he was standing right next to me, smiling as I pressed into his leg, holding my hand and giving me whispered words of comfort when I needed it. Just like I do to my sweet, scared little redhead.

On one of our recent conversations, Amy told me something that has stuck with me, something that I will treasure forever as a balm over some of my heart scars. She told me she was proud of me for *pressing in*. All those times over the last couple of years where I felt like I was losing my mind, myself, my husband, my family—she saw something I couldn't see in myself at the time. She saw that I ran to my Daddy, that I pressed in and wouldn't let go. That I was counting on him, putting all my eggs in his basket, so to speak, to bring me through all the hurt and pain and bewilderment and crushed expectations that I was experiencing.

The last few years have been trying in ways that are outside of my realm of experience, outside what I would've ever imagined our family could survive. And that little book I wrote before everything went to hell in a handbasket—a book about celebrating no matter what—was put to the test. My own words and thoughts were thoroughly tested.

I failed miserably some days.

I sat on that finished manuscript for over a year because I couldn't bring myself to publish a book about celebrating when my world was crumbling all around me. I couldn't even fathom the thought of the work it would take to pursue it. I was too tired from living. But God—our big and wonderful God—showed me how to celebrate in the middle of the mess.

Please excuse me because it gets ugly.

My husband went bat-crap crazy and had to go to treatment for over two months, so God gave me a baby in my belly that made me have to take care of myself instead of actively working to destroy what was left of my life. We had both a PTSD and traumatic brain injury (TBI) diagnosis. We got the happiest, most laid-back baby to bring our family back together again after it was nearly ripped completely apart. God gave us three other children who somehow thrived and were joyful and played basketball and won scholastic awards and had friends and played outside, running and yelling and laughing during this time, even when I was falling apart and my sweet Mr. Wonderful had been ripped to shreds by the Mad Cow monster.

God gave us friends and family to look after us. He somehow worked out finances, therapies, sobriety, groceries, traveling to see Mr. Wonderful in treatment, baby showers, medical military retirement, and doctors who cared. He got our family through the worst of the worst that I had ever experienced and made sure all of us were still standing. And he let me cling to his leg when I got scared, crying and screaming and throwing the mother of all temper tantrums, imploring him to not let go.

God took my pressing in and used it. He showed me how to be grateful during the pressing in, during the grief of watching a loved one walk to the precipice and lose his footing. Some days it was merely painting my fingernails and hoping for the best. Some days it was dancing with my pregnant belly getting in the way as I would spin my daughter. Some days it was watching my sons vie for who got to be the gentleman and open the door for mama. Some days it was quiet moments where I would feel the life growing inside me move and shift in response to my hand or my voice or my prayers. Some days it was just clinging, pressing in as gratitude.

Why choose gratitude? Especially when things are so out-of-control wrong that you don't know if you'll be able to take it? Because I have lost or nearly lost people and things and pieces of myself and how I thought things would be. Because every day that I wake up is one more God-given chance to get it right. Because my gratitude—unfettered and unleashed—puts my focus on a God bigger than I am, bigger than my problems could ever be.

For a clinger like me, gratitude is how I can let go of control and trust God, pressing into his presence because he is faithful to keep his promises.

Salt, Light, and Red Lipstick

This new normal is something else.

I never imagined in my wildest dreams that I would be living this life. At first, it was a beautiful and somewhat messy fairy tale—turned nightmare, turned rewritten, reimagined fairytale. In a short few years together, Mr. Wonderful and I have cobbled together quite a story.

It seems that by rewriting our story, our near end became our new beginning. Endings are sad. Scary. Sometimes lonely. They feel so final, like the words *The End* at the end of a story. I personally loathe endings. That is, until I remember that with every ending comes a beginning.

And I *love* a good beginning.

These are scary too. But in a different way. They're scary in a leap-as-you're-checking-for-a-net scary. They're exciting. They're chaotic. They're wonderful for a leaper like myself. I have found in the many leaps at the many beginnings that I have managed to live through, create for myself, or be invited into that chaos is the perfect place for reinvention—of self, of ideas, of a life that you always wanted to live but just haven't yet.

The reinvention of me has led me through several lifetimes. I have been a music minister, waitress, retail worker, returning college student, artist, writer, lawyer, mom, chauffeur, dreamer, worker bee, executive director, expectant adoptive mom, expectant pregnant mom, divorcee, newly remodeled bride. I've been in, shut out, applauded, laughed at, encouraged, and criticized. I've made friends and frienemies. I've made money and lost it. I've traveled and become a hermit.

At all these beginnings, even the ones that had bad endings, I've still had that sense of excitement, of possibility, the anything-could-happen-at-any-moment feeling that propelled me forward, good or bad. That hopeful feeling that things just might go my way or turn out better or take me somewhere I've never been has been at the beginning of my beginnings.

My short life with Mr. Wonderful has already seen so many beginnings and endings that, for a while, we were spinning from one change to the next, reeling like the scary Tilt-A-Whirl carnival ride we didn't want to get on in the first place. The last few changes are ones I would not have signed up for had anyone asked my opinion.

I never would have wanted Mr. Wonderful to have a debilitating disorder like the Mad Cow. If it were up to me, he would have gotten to continue his dream of being an army guy, putting in his twenty or thirty years and retiring at the top of his game. Neither one of us would have imagined that he would need a caregiver by the time he was thirty-five years old. I'm positive that you could never have convinced me of this when we first met. No way would my big, strong man with the heart of a lion ever need to lean on me.

This beginning is trying. Overwhelming. Butt-kicking. Quite often, I have no idea what I'm doing because all of this is out of my wheelhouse. It is out of the bounds of anything I have ever known. I am sure Mr. Wonderful feels some of these same things too. We flounder a lot because we have no idea where all of this is headed. We only have our very limited human worldview.

Some days are harder than others. Some days are just my red-lipstick days.

These are the days I wake up to a rougher-than-normal morning. This usually entails four children bombarding me with questions before I have even had a chance to take a sip of coffee. They should know better! This mama leads a highly caffeinated lifestyle, and we have the "don't talk to me until I've had at least one cup of coffee" rule at our house. A rougher-than-normal day usually means Mr. Wonderful has had a hard night with no escape from the torment of his nightmares, which means Charlie, the service dog (a.k.a. guardian angel) and I have been working overtime hours trying to calm him in his sleep. Thank God I have reinforcements now! Before Charlie, this used to be solely my job. In the middle of the night in a half-groggy state, I would have to decide whether or not to take my life into my own hands and try to use my body weight to comfort the giant man with the seventy-two-inch wingspan while he was thrashing about. There were no winners there, trust me.

When we all wake up discombobulated or late or tired or frustrated or all of the above, and things feel like they're slipping into that crazy place, the only things I know to do are pray and put on red lipstick. I wear my lipstick as a sort of armor, pushing back all the bad and ushering in the new. If you see me out and about wearing my red lipstick, know this: I'm wearing my war paint, and I'm ready for battle.

Today was a red-lipstick kind of day.

I was reading my devotional in the prekid hour, and of course, it was about being salt and light. I've read those verses many times, but today, everything came together in my mind about beginnings and salty flavor and hiding my light under a bushel (no!). It all swirled around my barely-firing neurons to lead me to some thoughts I have never had before.

Mornings are beginnings.

I like beginnings.

There are new mercies every day.

I can be salt and light to my family.

Mornings can be a time of salty new beginnings, lighted by Jesus' love in me.

My stream-of-consciousness thinking kept bringing me around to how I am behaving, how I am treating this new normal. I have been railing against what feels like God's radical plan for us. I have been standing on my tiptoes, trying to see the bigger view, the bird's-eye view, actually the God's-eye view. But only God, in his infinite wisdom and love and care for each detail of our lives, has this view. I've been trying to understand the whys and the hows when what I was really supposed to be doing is showing my family my salty flavor and shining a light into this new normal.

God's new mercies have been escaping my notice for far too long. I've been getting caught up in all the junk and mess and mud of the new normal rather than seeing each moment for what it really is: a new beginning. A new mercy. Another opportunity to be a smiler, an encouraging-word giver, a pat-on-the-backer, a knitter of wounds and emotions and crazy days and bittersweet memories. Ashamedly, I have been like the salt that lost its flavor and the light hidden away.

Oh.

Realizations that cause this level of self-introspection and correction are not my favorite. I often try to avoid them. This one was a doozy. I'm not responsible for everyone's happiness. However, I am responsible as one of the grown-ups in this house to help set the tone, especially if the other grown-up is having a tough time. And I'm the mama of the house. It is my job to show these amazing little humans how to grow into amazing big humans. How can they see if I don't help light their way?

Salt and light.

Hope and gratitude.

Progress by leaps and bounds or progress only by bits and pieces.

All of this comes only in God's time and in his radically different plan from the one I had picked out for myself. When Mr. Wonderful and I got married, I had a vision of how our new life together was going to look. Sure, it involved some hard times, but mostly it involved bliss and wonder and running through fields of daisies with my kids and Mr. Wonderful doing his much-loved military thing. You know, realistic stuff.

In God's plan—now that I'm not protesting—I get to minister to my whole family. In his plan, I get a new beginning, that thing I love every morning when I wake up. His mercies are there, just waiting for me to look their way, notice them, invite them in, bathe myself and my children and Mr. Wonderful in them, to take the servant's pose as Jesus modeled for us when he bathed the feet of his disciples.

I can add a salty flavor to the spice of my family's life just by embracing the beginning of each day. Renewing my spirit, taking time to get my mind and my face and my heart aligned before I speak one word to my family will help me blanket our mornings with peace and promise, not crazy and chaos, even in the midst of crazy and chaos. If I work on embracing the beginning—one of the things I actually crave in this life—I bless. I show gratitude by being thankful just to be given a shot at one more day. One more chance to make things right. One more opportunity to live out God's plan for me, whatever that is and wherever it takes me. One more day to celebrate because there are no throwaway days.

I've always been a big-picture kind of girl. Any time we go on a trip, I want to look at the map to get the full picture. I want to see point A and point B and what I'll be driving through to get to my destination. Mr. Wonderful is exactly the opposite: he just programs his destination in and takes the turn-by-turn directions as he gets them. This drives me crazy! What if the directions are wrong? What if Siri is leading you somewhere you don't want to go?

She's been wrong before, you know. More than once.

That is how I try to be with my life sometimes too. Occasionally I'm like, I just want to see the whole map, God! Then I could avoid some of those pitfalls and road construction and take the scenic route when the interstate becomes too boring. But that is not how he operates, not to frustrate us or cause us pain but to show that we can trust him. To show us that if we surrender to his sometimes turn-by-turn instructions, even if it seems like we are going the wrong way, his way will be higher than our way, his plan better than ours. With a little time and hindsight, we will see this. We will appreciate it as the blessing that it is. The big picture, the God's-eye view—that's no longer for me. That is for someone who is in control.

Not my plan but his.

Not my way.
Not my vision.
Just some salt and light.
And maybe some red lipstick.

Hot Mess

Is it weird that sometimes I just want to slow-motion walk through my house with dramatic music playing, wind machine whipping my hair gloriously behind me, while wearing some fabulously sequined outfit with a faux-fur cape parading my superpower as a mama?

Don't answer that. The heart wants what the heart wants.

Reality check: I am usually wearing my workout clothes, not because I have worked out but because I am still holding on to the sliver of hope that it will somehow happen, maybe while I'm not looking. Those workout clothes are probably stained with baby schmutz from earlier in the day that I have yet to notice. The hair is ponytailed or hatted to confine the curls. The children—well, sadly, the children take after their mama.

I love how Big Brother "matches" his clothes by wearing different hues of only one color. Usually the hues are superclose, making it appear that I am a horrible laundress, fading clothing left and right, which I am and I do, but he does not need to advertise it. Next in line is Little Brother, the kid who doesn't care if his shoes are on the right feet and has been seen wearing everything inside out and backward. My favorite is when he is wearing jeans wrong side out because the pockets are hanging on the outside like sad little puppy-dog ears.

Little Sister, the most fashion conscious of the bunch, will use her honestly inherited flair for the dramatic to combine costumes with cowgirl boots, skirts with jeans, turn dresses into shirts. Like her mama, she is not afraid of color, beading, sequins, or feathers—all at once.

Baby Houdini just wears what mama puts him in. For a while. Usually I turn around and he's somehow pantsless again, but it doesn't seem to bother him. He is just happy to be wherever the rest of his family is. In fact, he is just happy.

Even Mr. Wonderful is a bit out of sorts now that he has to wear civilian clothes. For a while, without the uniform, he was just lost. I have tried to increase his civvies, but I know he still misses not having to think about what to wear every day.

As I watch our children pile into our Suburban each morning in various stages of (un)dress, I am coming to the realization that I may have lost control of this Traveling Circus. Some weeks, it feels like I got run over by it, elephants stampeding, clown car spilling out the sides, ringmaster hiding in her closet because she can't find a thing to wear, acrobats refusing to perform. It's conversations like the following that convince me this is true.

Little Brother came to tell us the television was no longer working. When I asked him what happened, he replied, "Well, I was doing a cartwheel and...."

....

Sidebar: It's amazing how many stories of mayhem and destruction at my house start with that phrase.

....

This was also the week when Baby Houdini became especially adept at his escaping skills. No door, no bed, no room or confinement is safe anymore. How good is he? I put him down for a nap upstairs in his crib, and six and a half minutes later, I passed him strolling through the hallway downstairs. I did a double take. Uh, weren't you just taking a nap?

....

Second sidebar: A lot of things happen at our house when I think kids are napping.

....

From what I could piece together after interviewing the suspects and examining the evidence at the scene, Baby Houdini had enlisted an accomplice (Little Sister) to bust him out of baby jail (a.k.a. his crib). According to eyewitnesses, he used some sort of baby code to give his insidious escape plan to Little Sister. My crack team of code breakers have yet been unable to decipher it. Little Sis told me the baby made her do it. I halfway believe her.

The evidence of the escape is as follows: Next to the crib, there was a small rocking chair—*an unstable rocking chair!*—which apparently the thirty-four-pound redheaded she-child used to stand on to get her twenty-six-pound little brother out of his crib. Then, like she told me, he must have just climbed down the stairs by himself.

My heart was in my throat.

This same redhead, who shall remain nameless, was also recently found sleeping in a box. That's right, folks. Step right up and take a look at the redheaded she-child sleeping in a cardboard box even though she has a bed three feet away.

She has an imaginary best friend named Jake. From State Farm. I have actually said the following sentence: "If Jake from State Farm isn't in this car in thirty seconds, I'm leaving without him!"

Great marketing plan, State Farm. Thanks.

As if you needed more proof that the Traveling Circus might be short a trapeze or two, Little Brother told us five minutes before we walked out the door to his parent-teacher conference that he was "a little nervous" because he had not made good choices. Big Brother was suddenly concerned we would embarrass him by breathing and existing. As you can plainly see, this was a week where the Traveling Circus had more clowns than ringmasters.

I'm just going to put this out there: personally and professionally right now, I am a hot mess. As I have told both my board of directors at the Wegener Foundation and my family, I am currently drowning in children, work, responsibilities, and laundry. Things are a smidge out of control. A bit chaotic. A big, fat swirling mess. And I am scared that it is not just a temporary situation.

You see, I'm afraid we have turned into *that* family.

You know the ones I'm talking about. You have seen them before in restaurants, parks, shopping centers, and the like. They are noisy, unmatched, impossibly unorganized. There may be yelling and temper tantrums, dropped ice-cream cones and spilled milk, forgotten toys and stinky diapers. We have all seen them. And now that I am fairly certain I am part of *that* family, I beg you—look away.

Here's what the average Joe or Josephine does not see when they glimpse a sliver of our crazy. The big, strong man with the military bearing brought home a little souvenir from his overseas deployment we call the Mad Cow. The Big Brother is a natural-born caretaker, sometimes little old-manning his siblings much to their dismay, also possibly his mama. Little Brother has a bundle of energy that we have not learned how to harness yet because of some sensory and learning issues and ADHD, which translates into frustration, which may or may not lead to random outbursts of both noise and body parts from both him and myself, and probably Mr. Wonderful. Oh, and Baby Houdini. All right, all of us.

Little Sister is finding her place in our family. She is strong-willed and already more sure of herself than most grown-ups, which will be awesome when she's actually a grown-up but sometimes makes parenting her...

challenging. This is the girl who asked, "Where's my freakin' binky?" when she was just a wee little lass in front of several other moms who clearly disapproved of my parenting skills. She's the kid who said, "It smells like butt in here" in her mom's day out program. In her defense (and mine), she was right. It did smell like butt.

Baby Houdini has probably escaped and will be wandering around happily. He will smile and laugh and win your heart, only to give you a panic attack two minutes later because you are unable to get a twenty on him. Searching with panic rising, you will notice both he and the service dog have decided to take advantage of the beautiful day and sunshine by heading out into the parking lot. With no supervision.

And the mama? Well, she's just trying to keep her family together. You don't see how much she loves her whole family, so you might be tempted to judge her handling of the aforementioned tantrums or meltdowns. She might even throw her hands up in the air and have a tantrum of her own. I confess, sometimes I have a hard time with moments where I am supposed to be all Jesus-y.

Everyone in this kooky family is doing their absolute best almost all the time. So when we make mistakes, which we all do *a lot*, please give us a break. Understand that we are doing what we can in our given set of circumstances. We may, in fact, look insane from the outside. From the inside, though that is messy too, we are a family who laughs so much, plays so hard, loves so deeply. And though you may not see it, that is who we are at our core.

We have our together moments, and then we have our completely opposite fall-apart moments. If you catch us in the right moment—a rough day or a rough month or even a rough year (e.g., all of 2013)—you would be sorely disappointed in my parental management and coping skills. You might even think terrible things about me and wonder why I ever had kids.

But that is okay. I know I am doing my best, and I am keenly aware that my best doesn't quite cut it sometimes. The standards that I'm trying to live up to are impossible standards set by a perfect and holy one. I will fall short every time, every day, every minute. But that doesn't keep me from striving. I know I won't be able to attain perfection; but I believe in trying anyway, day after day, even when I make big, fat, colossally ridiculous mistakes.

I believe in making missteps.

I believe in falling flat on your face.

I believe in catching some heat, ruining your best shoes, spilling gunk on your white pants, getting your hands dirty, and generally making a mess of things. Because I know that if I have done any of that, it means at least I am trying. And the getting-up part after a mistake is often much more important than the failure part. It is in the trying again, the restart, the new beginning, the new mercies, the fresh slate, the grace that are the important parts of the mistake.

Without them, the mistake remains a mistake. A screwup. A mess. But with them, there is the possibility of glorious redemption and beauty from ashes. That means there was a purpose for our pain.

We are all a hot mess, but here is the best news ever. We can be Jesus' hot mess. All of us. He loves us *right where we are.* In our family, we have learned a few things by owning up to our hot-mess-ness. Real life breaks your heart. Real life wrings you out. It makes you delirious, sets you on fire, dumps you upside down. It is too exhausting trying to hide my family's crazy. I'm rolling my eyes at myself at the thought that I could even try. Those who know us and love us anyway know the extent of the weirdness at our house. But all of this is how I know to give you some encouragement. Some hope.

Has hope been rather elusive for you lately? Have you felt outcast, down, or alone? Maybe you're in a rough season right now. Maybe you've been in a rough season for some time, and you just need some relief. Maybe you're to the point where you have worn out your knees, and you think to yourself, *I can't handle one more thing*. And then one more thing happens.

I get this. You are not alone, my friends.

I have been in that season. The last few years of my life have been the most uncomfortable, wild, wonderful, and sometimes downright painful years of my life. But these years are how I know to give you some encouragement, some light for your darkness. They are how I know to tell you to just hold on. Hang tight. Take it from this hot mess—you are just around the corner from something amazing. You just have to trust that God, our Father, has gone *before* you, is *behind* you, and walks *beside* you. He will see you through this season.

How do you get through it, hot mess and all?

Celebrate.

Every day, even in the middle of the mess, find something to celebrate. Even if it is just that you survived the week until Wednesday, or that your shoes match, or that you had time to take a shower, or that your favorite lip gloss is on sale.

I believe that throwing a party—I mean, really celebrating deep in the core of your soul despite your circumstances—unleashes something powerful in heaven. The fact that you would celebrate in the midst of the good times or the fantastically screwed up shows faith in a big God.

I believe in looking in the mirror each morning that you have had the privilege of waking up and reminding yourself that today is a good day for a good day. At our house, we choose to celebrate the broken, the misfits, the weird, and the forgotten. We celebrate the different, the outcasts, and the abandoned. We do this because that's who we all are at our very center before Jesus gets ahold of us. That is the example he set for us when he walked this earth. He celebrated. He broke bread with his people, that crazy mismatched tribe. They were all broken in some way. They were *that* family.

I'm beginning to realize that the more broken we admit to being, the more room there is for God's light to work in us and shine through us. So here is a thought when you see *that* family: Be weird together. Own your crazy and celebrate your crazy just like they do, just like we do, because you—and they—are just right.

Foo Hands

News flash: I hang out with my kids a lot.

I work from home, so these munchkins are with me *all the time*, especially in the summer. Most days, I love this with my whole heart. I also unashamedly do my happy dance, and Mr. Wonderful will take me out to breakfast the first day that everyone's back in school and/or mom's day out. As I am trying to teach my kids to live in the *now* and celebrate the *now* (after I've had my first cup of coffee, of course), I have to do the same.

I haven't always been great at living in the *now*. When I adopted Big Brother, I couldn't wait for the next phase: crawling, walking, for the twos to be over, for the threes to be over, being potty trained, being able to dress himself. I was constantly waiting for the next thing to make me happy, bring me joy, fill me up.

I thought my schedule was so full that I couldn't handle one more thing. I laugh at my younger self now. One kid and law school was so hard at the time—I wasn't sure I would survive learning to be a mom while learning to be a lawyer. I had no idea what was to come. That's probably a good thing.

The current three-year-old—Little Sister—is one of my staunchest supporters and helpers. And often one of my biggest challenges. The aforementioned redheadedness combined with threeness is lovely and hard all at the same time. I adore that she is so sure of herself. At times, I'm pretty sure she has more confidence than me and the rest of the family combined, including our service dog. I want to foster and grow and encourage that.

I also want to scream.

This kind of absolute rightness that makes me smile in admiration and wonder can also simultaneously frustrate and confuse me. *Wait*, it has me thinking, *I thought I was the parent!* She is an adorable little bundle of awesomeness I could never have imagined. Like all my children, she is also an answer to prayer. Until kid number three, I never had the slightest urge for a she-child. After a long time of being afraid of being a girl mom, I actually begged God for one. I love that I'm a mom of mostly boys; but after two boys, I knew I needed my sidekick, someone who wants to do things like me, the one I can teach about girl things and lady things and womanly things.

Now that this little girl with the pretty heart and smart brains is among us, I am praying for God's hand to help me shape her in the right ways. I'm praying that I will be able to guide her without stripping her of that independent spirit. I pray I can show her how to respect others and honor her parents. As in—girl, sometimes just do what I say!

For instance.

We have four kids and three car seats when we go places. This means we need to have a good routine to get in and out of the car. If we didn't, we would never leave the house. I can somewhat go about normal, everyday errands, including taking all four kids with me to the grocery store. Our leaving routine includes Little Brother being on diaper-bag duty (ha, I said "duty" in this book too), mama getting Baby Houdini situated in his car seat, Big Brother buckling Little Sister, and everyone being responsible for their own drinks or snacks or toys—whatever they choose to bring on our adventure.

....

Sidebar: If you ever see me at the store with all four of my kids, please don't video us, snicker, or point us out to your family as what not to do. This is one of our most difficult feats as a Traveling Circus. This is our high-wire act where everyone is holding their breath. We are doing the best we can. There is no safety net.

....

When we get home, we reverse the leaving routine, and everyone is supposed to help carry in all the stuff they brought, plus the groceries. As most parents know, these kids brought enough stuff to go on a family vacation when we left the house. Books, teddy bears, sippy cups, pool toy (seriously? pool toy? we're not going swimming on our way to the grocery store!), dinosaur, and Lego™ set (don't even get me started on the number one cause of foot injury among parents) were somehow put in the car in case we needed them on our short jaunt.

If it goes in, it must come out. Our car has a tendency to be a record keeper of all the fantastic fun we've had, including ketchup stains to remind us of McDonald's, Magic Marker to remind us of mama's not-paying-attention-because-where-did-we-even-get-a-Magic-Marker, and a shirt that got wet and was forgotten until it was stinky.

The rule is, you have two hands, so you carry at least two things in. Most of my kids are pretty good about this, though the three-year-old she-child is still learning. She will hold her darling little purse in one hand and look up at me with her sweet doe eyes while she asks me to open the door for her. Meanwhile, I'm carrying seven sacks of groceries, the diaper bag that someone who shall remain nameless was supposed to get, and my giant-sized mama purse. I laugh hysterically at this point.

When I ask her why she can't open the door, she replies in all seriousness, "Mama, I have foo hands."

Of course you do.

You have your teeny tiny purse, and you're still navigating big-girl panties, and wearing clothes the right way and holding a purse and opening the door is *just too much.*

I get it, girlfriend.

Sometimes I just want to shout at God, *Don't ask me to do this—I have foo hands!*

I bet Jesus looks at us with the same tender amusement that I do with my kids. Like, *Aw, sweetie.* He pats our heads because we're trying so hard, and we think we have "foo hands." That's adorable. I wonder if he sees us struggling with what we think is just too much, and he quietly chuckles, knowing all along we just need to ask him for help with our heavy burdens. When we think we know all there is to know, when we have refused his help or pushed him away or shouted, "I do it myself!" is when he extends us the most grace, the most mercy.

Foo hands can happen to any person living on this planet. Anyone who's overwhelmed, overworked, underpaid, overtired, and just generally drowning will understand this. For every person who has ever felt completely vanquished by the life they're living, this is for you. Maybe it's not the downside of life that has you drenched and engulfed. Even good things like dreams and destinies and the desires that God put in your heart can feel daunting, overpowering, suffocating.

This push and pull, the tug-of-war between parent and child, is one I believe our Heavenly Father is very familiar with. He has given us free will to make whatever choices we think we need to make. He tries to mold us, shape us, and guide us without pushing his will or his way onto us. This Creator of all things could make us do what he wanted. He could force us to choose his way or be rough with us or run us over.

But he is a gentleman, instead choosing to love us and our foo hands.

He loves us through our stubbornness, even when we walk away from him. He supports us with his grace even as we curse his name. Sometimes he holds us, and we don't even know it—until one day we look behind us and can see all the ways in which he was shoring us up, anchoring us down from flying away, or walking before us to keep us from too much.

My advice to Little Sister when she says she has foo hands: put something down or give it to me.

You see, I believe she is fully capable of figuring out how to do this herself. I want to foster that independence, but I also want her to know I'm there, right beside her, should she ever need me because her burden is too heavy.

God sees our foo hands. He wants to love us into submission to him, where we willingly seek what he wants. He longs to empty your foo hands. You can either set stuff down or give the trappings of this life to him. If you're just trying to do too much for everyone around you, set something down. Give your foo hands a rest. Be particular about what you will allow to take up space in your life. Say thanks, but no.

If it's worries, ingratitudes, grudges, sins, hurts, regrets, and disappointments that are giving you foo hands, you don't have to hold them anymore. Those uglinesses that are weighing you down and keeping you from having hands open to receive his blessings can be given away to him, placed in his hands or at the foot of his cross. You don't have to bear those burdens anymore. You can empty those foo hands into his. Believe me, those scarred hands that were nailed to the cross *just for you* are big enough to handle anything you may need to put there.

All those gross, dirty, ugly things that you've been carrying around—dump them. Give them to the one who gives us the blessing of newness every day. Let the one who is Healer, Redeemer, Friend, Father, and Creator help you, guide you, mold you into the you that his destiny calls for. You won't regret it.

And you won't have foo hands anymore.

Who's Got This?

Do you know how unsettling it is to be double-checked by both a fifth grader and a three-year-old? I have two old souls among my children. They're both like oldest children, and in our family dynamic, they both kind of are. Big Brother, the fifth grader, is a true firstborn. He's the leader of all the other kids, very independent, analytical, a take-charge kind of guy.

Little Sister, the three-year-old is also like a firstborn. When the Bigs are at their dad's, she's the oldest kid in the house. She claims her role of firstborn as well, all the time, whether her brothers are home or not.

Both of these kids are constantly checking on me, like they think I don't have everything under control. I'm sure that, at times, it probably appears that I don't; but contrary to apparently popular belief, I usually manage. I think my fly-by-the-seat-of-my-fabulously-pink-possibly-bedazzled-pants makes them nervous. My artsy-fartsy attitude about everything makes them worry about me.

They worry about *me*.

Big Brother has a tendency to get wrapped around the axle on things that don't really matter. But then again, everything seems like a huge deal when you're a worrywart fifth grader. Like testing. They do this ridiculous testing for weeks in schools now, and it seems to stress everyone out, especially the more high-strung kids like Big Brother.

He's the kid who's worried about his permanent record.

Can we just have a quick discussion about this permanent-record thing? For years, I've heard this term bandied about as a threat, a coercion technique, a bribe. I have yet to actually see my permanent record on paper, or the Internet, or at any of the jobs I've managed to be gainfully employed at through the years.

This permanent record is confusing and elusive. I wish I would've known that it doesn't really matter when I was a kid. Just like Big Brother, I probably lived under the umbrella of stress about it when I was younger. In elementary, I was in a class full of boys at this little rural school. If memory serves, there were twenty boys and nine girls. In high school, I would've really liked those odds; but in elementary, it was terrifying.

All those boys together were apparently the exact combination of boyness to get our whole class in trouble. Constantly. And everyone—from gym teachers to music teachers to parents to principals—was always talking to our class about behaving, or our permanent records would reflect our shenanigans. This drove fear into my heart. My parents were teachers. They would see my permanent record and think that I was a troublemaker! Then I find out that the permanent record isn't really permanent.

That is all kinds of a paradigm shift.

You mean, no one's going to follow me to junior high then high school then college then grad school then my first job then law school and tattle on me? I would not have worked nearly as hard at hiding my infractions had I known this. Despite the permanent record hanging over my head for quite some time during my school career, I still managed to have probably too much fun. I was just sneaky about it. Do *not* tell my children this.

I tried to let Big Brother in on the inside info regarding his permanent record. It took some convincing, and we have had to do a lot of talking about things like testing. These conversations felt necessary because he needed to know that 1) he is loved, important, special, and amazing no matter how he does on a test; and 2) this test will not define him. Those are hard concepts to understand at this age when everything feels like a big deal.

I vaguely remember that phase. When I was about his age, I remember it being difficult to navigate my changing body plus all the hormones and expectations of others and myself. I used to put copious amounts of pressure on myself to be the best at everything all the time.

That's an exhausting life for a kid.

I try to handle these talks now with Big Brother with my usual grace, saying things like, "Lighten up, it's not the end of the world!" and then laughing like a maniac because that's exactly what my parents would say to me back in the day, and I would think, *You people have no idea what you're talking about!*

Sorry, 'rents.

I'm still learning how to be a parent to children who are exact opposites of me. Mr. Wonderful and I work well together because we are opposites as well, and I call on his logic and ever-present rockness in these situations. I worry about the fact that I may be stressing out Big Brother because he feels like he has to be the parent. How do you get a kid like this to just go with the flow?

Little Sister is also constantly checking on things. She asks one thousand times if I remember that I said she could have gum after school, or did I wash her favorite dress so she could wear it for the third day in a row, or that I will feed her and Baby Houdini.

In my defense, my children are always fed; and everyone, down to the baby, knows where the snacks are in the pantry: bottom shelf, easy to reach. Maybe I'm a little lax in constantly meeting each child's every need, but I figure, How will they ever learn to fend for themselves if they don't have to fend for themselves? Plus, I get in my weird time warp and don't realize it is way past time for the kids to eat. Around here, you know it is lunchtime when the baby is scavenging food from the floor and fighting the dog for crumbs.

We are a bit on opposite ends, me and these two precious kids. I adore them so much and want to hug and squeeze them. I want to laugh and dance with them. They will tolerate the hugs, but most of the time, they look at me with the crazy eye when I start dancing. They and Mr. Wonderful all gel so well together. They get each other, speak the same language, revolve on the earth's axis at the same pace. I am the faster-moving, highly caffeinated odd woman out, and these three often look at me with eyebrows raised in complete silence while I'm dancing.

I like to think I redeem myself when I come through for them time and time again, but I guess our journey has been pretty bumpy in the past, so they're not always sure of the driver. We've traveled an incredibly rough road the last few years, so I can't really blame them. Big Brother, the boy who hates change, has been witness to the most. He's the kid who remembers when his dad lived in the same house as him. He remembers the uncertainty of divorce, of a single mama trying to hold our little family of three together. He recalls meeting Mr. Wonderful for the first time and telling him, "You're not my dad, and you're bigger than a dinosaur!"

Big Brother is the kid who remembers changing schools and houses and the male presence in our home. He is old enough to understand that the Mad Cow is not pretty on hard days. He is an ever-growing time capsule of all my best moments and, unfortunately, some of my worst. No wonder this kid feels the need to confirm the fact that I actually know what I'm doing. Bless his heart, from his limited ten-year-old vantage point, things over the last few years must have appeared like they were unraveling faster than I could knit them together.

Sometimes they were.

This is why I always talk with Big Brother in absolute un-sugarcoated honesty. He has to know that I will always be there for him and I will always tell the truth, even if it's not what he wants to hear. I keep it age appropriate, but I won't lie. I can't. He needs to know that when things look like they're coming undone, they may actually be, but his mama is doing her best and relies on the only one who can see her through: her Heavenly Father. I hope my children can learn from my mistakes or the way things haven't gone the way I wanted or hoped or expected by seeing how I just surrender.

That's probably really difficult for them. These are my kids who try to parent me while I'm driving. Surrendering isn't in their nature. Are we going the right way? Did you remember the baby's sippy cup? Should you go this fast? You're driving really slow! Why are we stopped?

Or with homework: Are you sure that's the answer? That's not how my teacher told me to solve it. Why did you do it that way? Is that really how you spell it? What I want to say—okay, what I have said—is that I have more than a fifth grade education. In fact, I've been to *all* the grades, plus some. I've probably forgotten more than you have even learned at this point. I believe I *am* smarter than a fifth grader, to which there seems to be a lot of previously anticipated eye rolling and sighing.

My children haven't realized something yet: I have a different perspective.

Big Brother has his fifth grade know-it-all blinders on. He knows things because he can see them, or he has experienced them in a very limited way in his thus far sheltered life for the last eleven years, which is probably how I was at his age.

Hold on while I go call my parents and apologize.

He sees what *is*. He can't imagine what *can be*. Not yet anyway. He still has growing and maturing to do and, though I hate it, hard times to get through. These hard times or mistakes or leaps or choices that seem good at the time will be the things that shape him, smoothing down rough edges and grinding down the parts of him that aren't what will help propel him forward. The characteristics that will be honed by life's sandpaper will lead him through to God's destiny, his plan, his way for Big Brother to do life.

It dawns on me that I still have blinders on at times too. That I still need sandpaper. To fulfill God's plan for me—his special and uniquely Meredith plan—my rough edges need to be smoothed out. There are still areas that have a coarseness, a bristly-ness to them. I have whole spaces that are rocky and rugged, tangled and tousled, and that need work. Whereas God, in his infinite parental knowledge, has the big-picture perspective, I have my small-minded, shortsighted, and often small-hearted perspective. When I get caught in an inability to see beyond my current situation or double-check God with worry prayers (Are you *sure* you're on this, God? I haven't gotten an answer yet…), he probably smiles and patiently continues all of his behind-the-scenes work. He pieces me together in the chaos of my life, choices, and worries, and he won't stop until his good work is finished in me.

I get stuck in *my* way. Only life's difficulties and pressures have convinced me that surrender is surely the best option. Surrendering to my Jesus—the one who sees all of my sharp, ragged, unfinished edges and loves me anyway—is how I will survive. It's how I will persevere, and find fulfillment, both for my heart's desires, which God put in there in the first place, and for his way to become mine. Surrendering doesn't mean giving up power. It means gaining sight, losing the sharp angles and finding the softer, more pliable parts of me where God can really dig in and get some serious work done.

He does that for me, you know. He will do that for you.

And I'm grateful that he will do that for all my babies, no matter where that takes them or how he will choose to use them. Because these babies of mine aren't really mine. They're his. And just like I have to surrender myself to him, I surrender my children. My control. My will for their lives in exchange for his will.

As my kids watch me live a fully surrendered life—one that I confess I have to re-surrender every day because I forget that I don't *want* control—they will see how they don't have to parent me or worry about how I'm going to get things done or if they will happen at all. They will just see that Mama and her Jesus are truckin' along, and that he—not me—has got this.

Today

Please forgive me. I am feeling exceptionally human today.

I'm surrounded by boys. And children. And boy children. And a girl child who actually noticed mama was having a rough moment today, so she gave me three hugs, right before she took off with my ChapStick. That's almost as bad as walking away with my coffee.

Today I do not feel like dancing. I don't feel like smiling or encouraging anyone. I'm all encouraged out. Do you want to know how dire the situation really is? *I don't even have red lipstick on*. It's a red-lipstick kind of day, and I am wearing clear lip gloss.

I barely believe it myself.

Sigh. Make that a double sigh.

Today has felt like one delightful crap storm after another. I'm starting to wonder why in the world I am doing any of this. What's the purpose? Why parent these crazy children who can't be bothered to listen? Why caregive for a man who doesn't really want my caregiving today? Why try compassion or friendship or effort? Is any of this actually making a difference? The answer today feels like a big, fat no.

Anyone else have these days?

Just when I'm starting to feel my oats and really think I have a handle on things, we have a transition. Then there's a little adjustment time. Then crapstorm. I am seriously about to lose it today. Real and raw and emotionally wrung and wore smooth out. I am tired of trying to help everyone with everything and getting used up in the process. Do all mamas feel like this? Am I one ungrateful mother trucker even thinking this?

Probably.

There are just going to be days where I feel this way. I suspect where we all feel this way. I am going to put this out there right now: it is okay. If you are not feeling okay, that is okay. If you are a little cranky and slumming right along with me in your clear lip gloss, friend, we will survive. Whatever your day looks like today, it is okay.

Mine started out on a positive note. I woke up earlier than the kids so that I could be half caffeinated before the morning onslaught. Had some God time and did some writing. Then while they were enjoying a leisurely breakfast on their last day of freedom before school started, I took a quick bike ride around the neighborhood. Let me be clear: by quick, I don't mean I was riding fast. I just didn't ride long.

....

Sidebar: Every time I ride my bike down the slight hills of our 'hood, my legs pedaling as fast as they can so I can get up the approaching hill, I hear the theme song of the Wicked Witch of the West from The Wizard of Oz*—do do-do do-*DOO *do, do do-do do-*DOO *do. I wonder what this means.*

....

I then ran Big Brother, the newbie middle schooler, to his new school for a walk-through. Totally his idea to see where all his classrooms were and do a "dry run" of his class schedule. My first day of middle school was more like hours spent on an outfit then asking a lot of people where my next class was. His way may work better.

The impressive nugget of this part of the story is that I didn't even let him see me cry. My baby is starting middle school, and I can't believe it. The beginning of the end, if you ask me. I also got Little Brother to occupational therapy, had a pregrant site visit and meeting for my work, grabbed pizza, mailed some cards to some girlfriends, wrangled kids, did laundry, checked on everyone's clothing choices for the impending first day of school, and fussed with Mr. Wonderful.

Such good times.

I was highly productive, tried to encourage and keep my priorities straight. I really just needed a pat on the back or an "Atta, girl!" or a pep talk peppered with sentences like, "He is always going to be your baby," and "He will do great in middle school," followed by ice-cream sandwiches. But I didn't get that, so now I'm in a whole other room typing snippily. Never make a writer mad—it may go in her next book.

If I don't type snippily, I might use my typing words out loud. They used to be my driving words until I had kids, and then I decided maybe I should tone things down. So now when I have a rough day, I just type cusswords to my heart's content. And then I try to remember to erase them. I have to be careful if I leave my computer open since a full 50 percent of my kids can read.

Right now, I am just really ready to be somewhere else. Like, in life. I am ready to be further down the path of healing for the Mad Cow, so maybe I'm more wife than caregiver. I am so ready to understand ADHD and how to parent through it. I am ready to be a better writer and mom and wife—and beyond ready to have a handle on this raising-kids thing.

When is all this going to happen?

Do you ever have those times where you feel change is on its way? I feel as if there is a crossroads of some sort approaching. I think I smell change on the wind. We had a crazy day today. Of course, our family often does because crazy is our new normal, but I meant weather-wise. August usually contains what we 'round these here parts call the dog days of summer. The days that stretch out forever in a sticky, sweltering heat, raising blisters and baking car seats and making heat rise off the asphalt. But on the downhill slide of August, we experienced a fall day. The temperatures only reached sixty-four degrees, and I was wearing my jeans and a sweater.

I love me some fall. Oh, pumpkin spice and scarf wearing and cute boots and giant cups of coffee warming my hands and my heart—please hurry! I am in desperate need of my favorite season, and today brought me a much-needed taste. Today, just when I needed you, you showed up for a moment, and it made me excited and awed that you're truly, finally on your way.

Fall is a time of football games and leaves turning and outdoor smells like fireplaces and impending weather. Building nests of blankets and pillows while sipping my coffee and burrowing in with Mr. Wonderful sounds like heaven to me. I'm ready for several days in a row of crisp, cool mornings. I'm longing for the view outside my window to change to oranges and reds and yellows.

I'm sure we have more summer left. It wouldn't be Oklahoma if we didn't. I have loved this summer and even wanted to stop time for a bit during it, but now I could really use some fall. Around here, sometimes the change of seasons, instead of a gradual downshifting of one to the next, has more of a jarring-just-learning-to-drive-a-stick-shift feel.

Do they even make stick-shift cars anymore? I learned to drive on a four-speed 1977 Chevy Chevette with AM radio and a broken speedometer. I killed that car so many times when I was learning to drive it that we had to get a new starter. That's what happens when you let a twelve-year-old drive. Just kidding, I was fourteen. But the first time I drove a regular car was when I was twelve. That's how countryfolk roll. I'm now rethinking this idea as Big Brother rapidly approaches the countryfolk driving age.

The changing of seasons from hot, sticky sweetness to the comfort of fall is highly anticipated. I'm ready, but it's still August, and nothing comes before its time. God has been showing me that there are ways I can serve him with my time here on earth. There are some specific tasks that he is asking me to start checking off, and I have to be open to doing them. Living a full-on surrendered life is easy to talk about but difficult to walk on a consistent, daily basis. He shows me snapshots of things to come; and though they scare me probably more than I have ever been scared when it comes to career and following God's call on my life and having a servant mentality, I know that his way is mightier than mine.

My way is like the lingering end of summer, when it has already overstayed its welcome but *just won't leave*. It was nice and all for a while, but now everyone is so over it. Now it's just deflated inner tubes and sunscreen that someone left the lid off of and a pool that I'm pretty sure every kid in the neighborhood peed in. Forcing my way through life all heat and intensity and sounds of fireworks and kids hollering—I am so done with this. God's timing is ever perfect; and as I submit myself to what he wants to do in me and through me, the seasons will change exactly when they are supposed to and not a moment before, even as I try to bend them to my will.

Just like fall, whatever is next on the horizon will come into being at the right time and in the right way. Even if the changes are jarring, like that just-learning-to-drive-a-stick-shift feeling, bumping our way from one season to the next, getting a taste of the coming season only to find ourselves still stuck in the original season for just a bit longer. God loves us too much to let anything come before its time.

Even if I feel ready for the next thing, even if I long for the next thing with my whole heart and can't wait for it, there is a good reason, a God reason for its delay. I may never know what that reason is; in fact, the delay may not even be for me. The seasons will change when we have learned all we were supposed to and when we are ready for the next.

I have a feeling that my transition to my next season will be that jarring back-and-forth of the seasons. No graceful shifting from one to the next or clearly delineated lines. No, my transition will probably have some bumps, some wild and unpredictable shifts, some teases of what's to come only to settle back into the old season for a bit. But that's okay with me. Just like that wild-eyed fourteen-year-old driving a stick shift around on a parking lot, not yet getting the hang of the gas and the clutch working in tandem, hanging on tight to the steering wheel as the car *huh-huh-huh*s its way to either dying or second gear, I'm shifting my heart and my perspective and my timeline to God's.

That's all I want and nothing more.

High Heels and Combat Boots

Coffee Is My Love Language

I had a brilliant idea once. I thought it would be fun to take our entire Traveling Circus to my book-release party. We bring our own special brand of crazy—ain't no party like a Traveling Circus party. It should tell you a lot about our family that Baby Houdini is the easiest one to take anywhere.

Getting *My Pink Champagne Life* published is one of the top seven best moments of my life. After laboring in love for about a year, sitting on the book for another year while our lives fell apart, then finally searching for and finding a publisher, holding my actual book in my hands was a moment that made me need take a moment. The icing on my cupcake, so to speak, was to have my book-release party at Cuppies & Joe, my favorite cupcake and coffee house, where I wrote a large portion of the book.

The day of the book-release party, there was a flurry of activity, mostly because we have four kids and I still had to work since it was a Tuesday. Forty-five minutes before we had to leave, the frenzy was building because I couldn't figure out what to wear. It had to be pink, dangit! I also realized, rather belatedly, that I had no idea what went on at a book-release party—mine was the first one I would be attending. As I multitasked googling what to do at a book-release party while standing in my closet hoping for inspiration to strike, Little Sister found me.

At first glance, I had a heart-in-my-throat moment because I thought she was bleeding. Turned out, she just wanted to "be pretty for Mama's book party" and had taken my fave red lipstick and painted—her face, our couches, the carpet. So while throwing a tantrum (me, not her) that I couldn't find anything to wear, and instead of figuring out what to do at a book-release party, I began googling how to get red lipstick out of carpet and upholstery.

....

Sidebar: Rubbing alcohol or white vinegar will do the trick. I'm writing this down as the Lipstick Debacle of 2015 won't be the only time I need this information. Perhaps some of you have budding graffiti artists in your families as well.

....

Rough start. The only thing that got me through was knowing I was going to have two of my most favorite things soon: coffee and cupcakes. Though I never figured out what we were supposed to do at it, the book-release party was fantastic! Our friends and family took time out of their busy lives to celebrate with us, drink coffee with us, visit and watch my Traveling Circus perform. Mr. Wonderful kept me in coffee and cupcakes so I could chat with each guest who stopped by. Cuppies & Joe went above and beyond and created mini-pink champagne cupcakes just for the day. That party is now a very special memory.

Coffee isn't a new obsession for me, so it was fitting that I have my party in a coffee shop. When I was a kid, my Grandpa Clyde tried to deter me from drinking the stuff by telling me it would put hair on my chest. As a lady, I'm grateful he was wrong about that. Coffee is a necessity for me, kind of like breathing oxygen or leopard-print strappy sandals or Netflix. Coffee is how I survive the trenches of motherhood—we are outnumbered by our children, and for some reason, they always need me to do things for them. Coffee helps me act like a grown-up, and I deal with the chaos and the Mad Cow much better with it.

After five years of marriage and a ridiculous amount of coffee, amazing memories, dramatic moments, and hard times, I feel like Mr. Wonderful and I are coming into something really beautiful again. In the beginning of our beginning, our new life together was such a dream. We met through ballroom dancing of all things, and we were inseparable. We danced, we fell in ooey-gooey love, and we lived a fun, fast-paced social life with friends and family.

Our courtship was particularly squishy. We both oozed love for each other; the stuff was coming out of our pores. We were disgusting, at least that's what I've been told. I was a prepackaged deal: when we got married, I had two little boys ages six and two who came along with me. That didn't faze Mr. Wonderful. One of the things that drew this rainbows-and-butterflies girl to the type A military guy was his stability. His strength. The rock-steady way he wanted to care for all three of us.

I fell in love with the fact that he took out my trash and cleaned up kid or dog vomit and took kids to soccer practice and still opened my door for me. I couldn't get enough of the handsome, tough army guy who cooked and opened up his heart to me and had been at the same job for over a decade.

Steady. Stable.

After we had been dating about six months, my strong and handsome soldier guy got asked to sing the national anthem at the opening night of the Professional Bull Riders rodeo. On Valentine's weekend. Don't be jealous, ladies—I know it's secretly every girl's dream to spend Valentine's Day at the rodeo. If you don't know anything about rodeos, let me tell you it is a big freakin' deal to sing the national anthem at the PBR. This is the Cadillac of rodeos. Mr. Wonderful would be singing in front of about fifteen thousand people. No pressure. Before the rodeo even started, loud music accompanied the soldiers rappelling from the ceiling of the arena, and the ground erupted in flames as the letters *PBR* were lit on fire. We were treated to quite a show!

Can I just tell you that Mr. Wonderful has a gorgeous voice? He could sing my grocery list, and I would find it sexy. The night of the rodeo, he was really nervous, but he did it. He sang the national anthem in a huge arena with Jumbotrons and anxious cowboys and spotlights. He did a great job and started the night's festivities right—what's more patriotic than a soldier singing the national anthem? Afterward, we got to sit in the VIP section at the rodeo to watch the rest of the competition. This is to say we were literally close enough to the ring that it was a distinct possibility we would be christened with bull snot. And flying chunks of dirt. At least I'm hoping it was dirt.

Mr. Wonderful still seemed a little nervous, but as he had just sang in front of a huge crowd in a huge stadium, I figured he was due a little anxiety. There was so much going on around us, and I was just trying to avoid the rodeo clown heckling people in the crowd during the commercial breaks.

I'm usually not a fan of clowns, but I was comforted by the fact that this rodeo clown wore minimal face paint, and he had no balloon animals or honking noses in sight. Plus, during the rodeo, I watched him put himself in harm's way again and again to rescue the cowboys who had the misfortune of getting catapulted to the ground—and then being charged by a large hulking beast of a bull while they were still just trying to get their bearings.

During one commercial break, after good-natured ribbing of some of the crowd, the rodeo clown was suddenly in front of us, talking to Mr. Wonderful. I looked at the clown. I looked at the Jumbotron. I looked back at the clown. I could see myself on the giant screens!

And then he handed the microphone to Mr. Wonderful.

At this point in the story, I confess I was a little slow. Mr. Wonderful started talking into the mic like he had prepared for this moment, and then I—oh…wait…what's he saying? As he got down on one knee and whipped out a pretty little box, I suddenly became a blubbering, speechless mess on the Jumbotrons. I still have no idea what Mr. Wonderful actually said, except for the part where he asked me to marry him. I was barely able to get out a yes and a head nod before the crowd erupted into cheers.

Not many gals can say their marriage proposal involved a rodeo clown.

Magical moments like my rodeo proposal and our Wednesday morning wedding and finding out we were pregnant immediately after we got married and taking the honeymoon trip of a lifetime and loving the new family we had created and making memories and becoming lake people made me feel as if I had stepped into a wonderful, messy fairy tale. Things didn't always go as planned, but they were beautiful and golden and light.

Those aren't the times that made us strong, though. As anyone who has lived for a while can attest to, mountaintop moments (even highly caffeinated ones) don't last forever. The hard moments, the dark seasons where things are dying left and right—those are the times that make or break you in a marriage. The journey to a PTSD diagnosis, figuring out how to live and love through the Mad Cow—these steps and missteps along the path are what made me know Mr. Wonderful was a keeper. And that I was stronger than I ever imagined.

I knew from the beginning that I married a good guy. But our love in the beginning of our beginning had only been tested by small events and minor moments. We hadn't felt the weight of soul-crushing burdens together yet. We had blended a family, and that went better than we could have ever imagined. We moved to the country and found ourselves the proud owners of five whole acres that we had no idea what to do with. We walked through an asthma diagnosis, a lawsuit, and the deaths of my beloved Grandpa Stanley, Oscar the Wonder Dog, and my Great-Aunt Francis.

We thought we had been tested and won.

The more difficult and true tests were about to come, and if I am completely real with you, we sometimes failed. In many ways. We panicked, and we made decisions based on fear, and we hurt each other and our family. We had no idea that the journey through the Mad Cow would be so long and hard, mostly because, at the start, we didn't even realize Mr. Wonderful had the Mad Cow. It's difficult to prepare yourself for something you don't even know exists.

We were a happy family with a beautiful beginning when the flames of PTSD began to lick at the edges of our home, threatening to consume it with a five-alarm blaze before the smoke detectors even went off. We began inhaling smoke as we tried to feel our way out of our burning home, and we lost sight of each other. I went one way, and Mr. Wonderful went the other. We had no escape plan for this. It was happening, and there was no plan.

There is no handbook on how to survive the Mad Cow with your marriage and family intact.

We knew from the beginning of us that we needed Jesus at the center of us. We thought he was. We assumed he was because we prayed and went to church and gave our tithe. What we found out during the fire was that our focus had been on each other, not him. And when you take your eyes off Jesus, your whole house can go up in flames pretty quickly, with you still trapped inside. We almost succumbed to the fire.

All the junk that you bring with you into your house makes pretty good kindling.

Even after the flames are extinguished, everything smolders for a while. The destruction is hard to look at because it's your memories and expectations that got all burned up. There are ashes left behind that no one knows what to do with, and you both get covered in soot if you decide to stay and rebuild. That's what Mr. Wonderful and I decided—we would stay, and we would rebuild. Even if it was messy and time-consuming and felt nearly impossible.

This was a decision reached in the most unlikely of places: rehab. After those terrible tree-house moments, Mr. Wonderful went to treatment with others just like him, military heroes who had just had too much. Too much of not being able to cope with what they had seen and done for their country, too many bad feelings, too much alcohol, too many prescription drugs, too much of the military telling them to soldier on when no more soldiering on was possible.

On one of my early visits—when my burns were still tender and healing and I felt broken by the weight of being pregnant and handling our life by myself and worrying about Mr. Wonderful and wondering if he would ever be the guy I married again—he and I had a real heart-to-heart. We realized that we could not go back to who we were or how our marriage had been. Our life could not be the same because Mr. Wonderful was not the same. Neither was I. After surviving the fire that nearly consumed us, we could only move forward and rebuild. Backward to our still smoldering, destroyed home was no longer an option.

Rebuilding meant making changes and allowances for this new diagnosis and new sobriety. The Mad Cow would not win, but rebuilding our family would take time. We had to get medicines and therapies correct and consistent. Ironically, I had written a book with *champagne* in the title, and now we were going to be a sober household. There would be times when our baby coping skills would be overwhelmed by the veracity of the Mad Cow and the struggles of alcoholism. We would not know what to do or how to do it most of the time for a while. We had to make some new promises, some new marriage vows to each other. They were very simple really: Jesus would be in the middle of us. We would not leave. We would give each other a break.

We have come a long way from that rehab hospital in Texas that helped us start rebuilding our foundation. We have learned to laugh and love each other in new and meaningful ways. We don't get out to the rodeo these days; we don't get out much anywhere anymore. But we give each other a break. A lot. We talk to each other when we are having hard days. If there is a moment of joy to be had, we revel in it, relishing each second so that we can build up piles of joyful memories to help us when things get tough again.

The little things matter at our house now; we don't dare take them for granted. We extend kindnesses over and over again because those little things matter so much. One of the sexiest things Mr. Wonderful does for me now is prepare my morning coffee the night before. This ensures I have coffee when I wake up superearly to handle our chaotic mornings. He knows this helps me function as a mama so I do not crush our children like bugs. No matter how his day has gone or how he feels, he consistently empties out the old coffee grounds and makes sure some strong coffee is waiting for me the next day.

I now let him sleep through our chaos of the mornings. One of my gifts to him is handling the morning crazy so that most of it is finished when he wakes up. Sleep and peaceful wake-ups do wonders for the Mad Cow, we have discovered. Mornings are the hardest part of the day for my soldier. The nightmares he's battled all night long leave him exhausted and disoriented when he wakes up early, so I let him sleep and miss most of the hustle and bustle. Every day we get better at listening to each other and filling each other's love tanks in the ways that we each need to be loved.

Because our house burned to the ground, we had to rebuild to suit our new needs. Our new normal. This could only happen because we pray. We care. We listen. We make each other coffee. We mess up. Sometimes we try to go back to the burned house. The old ways. The former expectations. And when one of us tries to go back, we show each other grace and remind ourselves that this is our new life.

Day after day, rebuilding first our foundation with Jesus then our relationship with each other, we grow stronger and better. Our house is on a much firmer foundation than the one that burned. Our wounds are healing, we are taking care to treat them, we are learning to live with and love through the Mad Cow. Now our marriage is a lot like that coffee that Mr. Wonderful makes for me every day: put us in some hot water, and you'll see how strong we really are.

Fifty Shades of Crazy

Faking it.

That's what I did for a long time when the bottom dropped out of our lives. I faked optimism and hope and joy because I believe in the whole "fake it 'til you make it" phenomenon. I've been faking it for a while now, though.

There are days when it all comes apart; and pretty soon, if those days string into weeks or months or years, you can start to feel a little like a fraud while you're faking it. You feel like a liar, like an imposter.

My cup of optimism has overflowed my whole life. It was always so full nothing could get me down. Not failures or embarrassments, not divorce, not being a single mom. I had so much of the stuff I poured it out on everyone around me because I had plenty to go around. When I didn't have the optimism, I faked it. And then I didn't have to fake it anymore because good times followed: falling madly in love, getting married, having babies. Overflowing again.

And then bad things happened, followed by more bad, followed by the unbelievably worse. A full couple of years of pain and heartbreak. As we were scrambling to right our life that had burned to the ground, my rose-colored glasses got stepped on and broken in the melee. My rainbows were obscured by storm clouds, and my butterflies hadn't come out of their cocoons yet.

I got really tired of faking it.

Our life and the weight of my responsibilities closed in on me like the walls of a prison. I felt trapped by our circumstances; and it seemed like everything I did, all the actions I took to change our situation and improve myself and our life, did not budge where we found ourselves. The first year after the PTSD diagnosis and treatment, I was exhausted and overwhelmed, working three jobs and raising four kids, sometimes by myself. I was barely hanging on. Mr. Wonderful was still trying to find his footing. He was exhausted and overwhelmed by the Mad Cow, the therapies, the medicines. We were fighting the VA when honestly we had no more fight left in us. I was running so fast. If you ever see me running, you better start running too. As a rule, I don't run unless something large is chasing me. I was exhausted from trying and striving and doing it all.

Until I couldn't.

I was a fraud, and I just couldn't do it anymore. I told Mr. Wonderful I was near the edge of the cliff and I just could not go on like this. I didn't want to. I was too tired.

Mr. Wonderful's response: he told me I should go to Bethel. Don't worry, that's not code for anything dirty.

We heard a sermon the day before all my crazy glue stopped working about how a man in the Bible named Jacob returned to Bethel some twenty years after he had first visited. When he was there the first time, he had changed the name of this sacred place to *Bethel*, which literally means "house of God" because that's where he had encountered God. In the story, two decades later, he goes back as a remembrance of his encounter with the Holy One. Turns out, remembrance is the most repeated command in the Bible. Apparently, taking time out to remember is a big deal.

Maybe Mr. Wonderful was on to something. He was gently reminding me to recall where I have met God, where I have been in his presence.

Big surprise that I was in a coffee shop when Mr. Wonderful texted me this advice. And there, drinking a large coffee with plenty of cream, I finally stopped faking it. God met me—this imperfect, whiny, often ungrateful little punk of a woman—right there in that coffee shop with his love and his grace. The people around me were probably wondering why the girl in the corner was blubbering away while she was scribbling notes.

I was trying to get it all down. My remembrance. My Bethel. I am so overwhelmed by awe and wonder that the God who manages the chaos of the universe and the flawed humans who inhabit a portion of it cares about each one of us. He knows the hairs on my head, the missteps of my feet, the desires of my heart. His joy and his peace are the way to fill my cup to overflowing again.

When I stopped striving and pushing and pulling and faking to become real and raw—less supermom trying to do it all and more alter-ego regular girl—God met me. He comforted me. He showed me that he would keep working on me and with me to accomplish his destiny for me. He reminded me that I wasn't alone.

He also called it to my attention that though our marriage relationship has changed, Mr. Wonderful was still my soul mate. That despite having lots of kids and jobs and responsibilities, the three of us—God, Mr. Wonderful, and I—are still in this together. That we are still meant for each other. That God gave us to each other and that we need to choose each other. Still. Every day.

Relationships are hard like that.

You have to wake up and choose love. Every day. Sometimes all day long. Sometimes minute by minute. Love between two people doesn't just happen and stay telenovela hot by itself. If that were the case, I would wear way more eye makeup, have big(ger) hair, and a much more fabulous shoe collection.

Real love, the kind that God had in mind when he created Eve to go with Adam, isn't all clothes-ripping romantic. You think Adam and Eve were all over each other after getting kicked out of paradise? That they couldn't keep their hands off each other after the downfall of humans into sin? My guess is that things were pretty frosty for a while. I am willing to bet that they fought and got mad and blamed each other all over again for the predicament they found themselves in before they ever had makeup sex. Probably even the first couple had trouble keeping the romance alive.

Sometimes people give up when real love gets messy. If it's done right, real love is actually a terminal condition. Vows said before God and friends and family are sacred. I have yet to hear nuptials include vows that use conditional words like *if* and *only when*. Most vows include something like, "'Til death do us part."

Like I said, terminal.

Messy.

Tattered, stained, and torn by the time it's all said and done.

It's not all rainbows and butterflies, romance and chocolate. Real love isn't a freaking Hallmark card.

Real love is hard-core choice. It's down and dirty because life happens. It is over-the-top holding on with both hands because the circumstances of the world threaten to rip you to shreds. Real love is joy, pain, hot, cold, right, wrong, and together alone. Real love is hard then easy then hard again. Real love, the kind that's terminal, is sexy even after sixty years of fighting, loving, and trudging through the mud and muck of life, still holding hands and trying to help each other up when your galoshes get stuck.

Real love makes time for each other, even when you're up to your eyeballs in responsibilities. Time alone is difficult to come by when there are lots of kids under one roof, one of you has the Mad Cow, and the other one is running around like a chicken with her head cut off. We have a whole barnyard thing going on over here. It's *really* real.

Through all the changes of the last few years, we have had to find new ways of romancing each other. Mr. Wonderful buys me coffee. Often. He knows this will bring a smile to my face and the caffeine will make my heart soft and sweet again. And when he needs to disconnect, robot-ing through his day, I give him time alone to find peace and quiet so he can tamp down the noises in his head.

Mr. Wonderful is slowly repairing my rose-colored glasses for me. He is a big fix-it guy, knowing his way around tools and garages and manly work. My glasses got pretty busted up, and tiny pieces went flying everywhere. He is carefully and methodically putting them back together, broken piece by broken piece, lovingly repairing each chipped section.

When his rough mornings turn into rough days, I am the perspective giver, the paradigm shifter. Our romance now includes my reminders to him that we know what to do with rough days and that they are only temporary. That the battles he is facing are not nearly as big or hard or scary as the battles we've already won. I remind him that we're in this fight together and that I'm his battle buddy now. I've got his six.

He takes me on weekly date nights, even though leaving the house is often difficult for him. We may eat dinner in a darkened back corner at 4:30 p.m., but we are out and we are alone, reconnecting and finishing sentences and laughing and renewing. That's how we do real love and romance now.

The Mad Cow and romance should not occupy the same sentence, but we are rebels like that. Having an invisible injury is hard on both the injured one and on the caregiver. Our love story, our messy fairy tale, is only partly finished. God put us together to help each other, complement each other, learn to lean on God to help us love and forgive another human being every single day of our lives.

That's what real love is: loving and forgiving every day—then waking up and doing it all over again, even when you don't feel like it. Real romance is holding your loved one's hair while they puke their way through chemo. It's cleaning up their messes for the four thousandth time. It's forgiving the hurts, big and small, that happen when two people merge hearts.

Sexy is showing up, giving grace, extending mercy.

Real love comes from going to Bethel, over and over again. Remembering, allowing yourself to be reminded of the place where you started and how far you have come. It's saying sorry or bringing coffee or reminding you to take your meds or grabbing each other's hands or butts. Real love is a gift from God between two imperfect people who put him first and each other second. *No matter what.*

Sometimes real love is hard and chaotic. Sometimes it's rainbows and butterflies. Real love is for realsies. It's TLC and PTSD and propping each other up. It is painful and wonderful all at the same time. Real love is having each other's backs, putting up with each other, choosing each other every day, and never giving up. Real love doesn't leave a man behind. Real love is fifty shades of crazy, but it's not fifty-fifty. It's 100 percent all in all the time. And if you happen to find it, hold on to it with both hands and don't let go.

Leftovers

Dinner together at our house is a regular and noisy affair. We all sit down most nights of the week and eat together. The kids don't know it, but this is my supersecret stealth plan to help them grow into amazing human beings. Please don't imagine for one second that our table is full of silverware and expensive china. We don't have stemware. There are no flowers on the table, and we're lucky if everyone has washed their hands and is wearing pants. Our table isn't fancy; and goodness knows, if mama's in charge of the cooking, we'll probably be eating takeout. But it is a time where we all sit down together with no technology and no interruptions, and we break bread and listen to one another.

This isn't easy when you have four kids ages ten and under—or let's be real, when you have any kids. Dinnertime is often full of "stop touching me" or "he licked my food" or "for heaven's sake, chew with your mouth closed."

One thousand times.

Sometimes Mr. Wonderful and I catch each other's eyes over the food fight being attempted by Baby Houdini, the two middle kids duking it out over who spilled the milk, and Big Brother's incessant tales of *Pokémon.*

"Tell me more about *Pokémon*," said no mama ever.

We just have to laugh and roll our eyes at the insanity of trying to have dinner together. It would be easier to just make TV dinners and have everyone veg out in front of the television and not speak to one another. Believe me, I'm tempted. But there are some moments—if I hold my head just right and take a second to breathe these babies in—that I actually feel the shifting and changing and growing of their bones and minds and hearts. It comes in waves, and it might be all four of them at once, or it might just be one or two of them. With each passing dinner, I know I am experiencing the last moment where they will be exactly that age. That way. Think those thoughts, say those words.

Every time I stop to think about this massive passing of time where we are all but grains of sand, I will myself to slow down. My babies—though they will always be my babies, much to Big Brother's chagrin—are going to go out into the world and have dinner tables of their own someday much too soon. And I will be left with a giant table that is empty. And quiet. And clean. As Mr. Wonderful already knows, I will hate it.

I love the chaos and the crazy of my family most days. Of course, there are days where I'm tearing my hair out or rolling my eyes at myself because life just could not get weirder. But those dinnertimes—even with all the circus folk trying to talk at once and with their mouths full—are precious to me. My hope is that when they have their own dinner tables and their own babies and their own observances of the passage of time, that they will take time for dinner together. That they will step away from whatever pulls them apart from one another and join hands to bless the food. That they will show their babies how to use napkins and where to keep drinks so you don't spill it for the third time in one meal, even as they are all eating while talking over one another with mouths full.

I pray for connection with my kids before they are all pulled hard in a million different directions. The day is coming; I can already feel its approach. Big Brother starts middle school soon, and that's a whole other planet to navigate. That is where friends become more important, peer pressure gets more intense, and sometimes Jesus gets replaced. My prayers and my dinner table are my two best weapons against all this.

I figure if we can sit down together as we have for several years now, pray, eat, and talk, good things will come from this simple act of breaking bread. Above the din and noise, I'm hoping I will hear other things too: fears that people won't like them, trouble with a bully at school, unfortunate incidents involving tripping in front of cute girls. I pray that we have created such a place around that table that guts will spill right along with the milk.

We have a good system down now. If he feels up to it, Mr. Wonderful and I usually take care of dinner, preparing an enormous amount of food to feed our family. Then afterward, the kids are on kitchen duty. They load the dishwasher, clear off the table, put the leftovers in the fridge.

There aren't many leftovers anymore because our kids eat like they don't know when their next meal will be.

Usually, the only time off from our family dinners is date night. This is a special ritual that I learned from my grandparents. Some of my favorite memories of them were their Friday night date nights, and Mr. Wonderful and I have instituted that same sacred ritual. Why? Because we have enough kids that finishing a conversation feels like climbing Mount Everest without oxygen or Sherpas, and because we want to keep liking each other. We want to continue knowing what the other person is thinking and feeling, and it's hard to get a handle on that around our house. Each Friday night, we get showered and changed into clean clothes that aren't pajama pants. I spend time on my makeup; Mr. Wonderful puts on his smell-good. We get excited to leave the house together. Alone.

And we talk. We laugh. We have conversations that have been on the back burner all week because there were some days where we couldn't fit a word in edgewise before falling into bed, exhausted. We reconnect with each other and remind the other person why they liked us in the first place. We flirt. We eat dinner by ourselves. This is glorious in the midst of the hard work that has been taking place all week. The Mad Cow alone would be tiring enough; but throw in going to therapies and doctor's appointments, wrangling kids at the dinner table, doing homework, making sure kids have had baths and brushed their teeth and said their prayers and cleaned their rooms, and giving them time-outs and removing privileges and building character, and of course, doing laundry and working—and you may find yourself at the end of your rope.

By Friday, we're exhausted. Date night would sometimes be easier to skip after having a particularly rough week. Sometimes we have skipped it. This is followed by intense regret the following week because we are all off as a couple. We're not ourselves. We haven't connected to each other so we could be a united front and friends and lovers. This is why it's imperative that after giving our kids our best all week, we turn around and do the same for each other.

For date night, we almost always go somewhere that serves big portions. I call Mr. Wonderful the leftover king because he's great at finishing the leftovers. By the time I remember we had leftovers and develop a craving for them, they're gone. This happened on our very last date night. We had a gift card to a fancy schmancy place that used actual tablecloths instead of paper ones you could draw on and cloth napkins instead of the paper ones I stuff in my purse because you never know when you'll need some napkins.

Except that I do know, and it's all the time.

This restaurant is someplace we would never go on our own. We would have to sell one of our kidneys or our kids to afford it. Since we had the gift card, we thought we should go and enjoy a nice dinner. It was wonderful, like when we were first dating and had a little more disposable income. We sat right next to each other in a booth. We ordered calamari and steaks. It was one of the best meals we had in a long time.

And of course, I'm such an amateur. I fill up on bread and calamari before my steak gets there, so fourteen ounces of rib eye is entirely too much for one sitting. After our meal where we talked to each other and I actually heard Mr. Wonderful belly laugh pretty hard (a rarity some days), we had our waiter box everything up so we would have leftovers later. The following evening, when I had a hankering for steak, I went to the fridge and looked everywhere for my leftovers. They were, of course, gone. I'm just not fast enough.

Some weeks, our kids don't get our best. And Friday date night rolls around, and we don't have enough left in us to give each other our best either. But that's okay. We are trying to give each other more than just the leftovers on most days. In every family, there will be ways that you have to shortcut or weeks that you just can't do any more because life and work and bosses and mortgages and bills and unexpected fires or emergencies or health issues have sucked out all of your physical energy and most of your mental and emotional energy as well. Those weeks are the weeks where you should give yourselves a break.

Just make sure that you don't let those weeks stretch into months, which stretch into years. Then one day you wake up in a place you don't recognize next to a person who has become a total stranger, and you no longer have your kids as glue. I don't know for sure, but I imagine that giving each other only the leftovers year after year could be a recipe for transitioning from friends and lovers to roommates. Sure, there are some times in a marriage where the leftovers are all you have to give, but too often, those times become seasons that become tradition. And it's really hard to break tradition.

Whenever Mr. Wonderful and I have gotten to the end of the week and the end of our rope and stayed in by ordering Chinese and watching Netflix as our date night, it just isn't the same as getting dressed up for each other and leaving the house together. Our relationship pays for it. We are edgier with each other, crankier. We don't show as much grace or overlook each other's flaws and mistakes and foibles. After a few weeks of this, rest assured we are ready to duke it out.

This is why we do our best to maintain date night as sacred couple time. *Commitment, faithfulness, servanthood*—these are all church words. But these could be couple words and date-night words too.

When we declare ourselves out on date night and present ourselves as a couple to the world instead of weary, harried parents, our relationship flourishes. When we give our spouses our best on a regular basis, good things happen. He or she will begin to look at you with a twinkle in their eye instead of a glazed-over look. Your spouse will see you. I mean, really look at you instead of through you. Your relationship, even if only one of you is currently giving your best, will change for the better. I am convinced of this. It's difficult for one person to constantly be the recipient of great things without soon bringing their own A game. When you give more than leftovers, you start getting more than leftovers.

I think God appreciates more than our leftovers as well. He is so good and loving that he actually enjoys his children and wants to spend time with us. He will even appreciate your leftovers. But how much fuller and richer would a relationship with the God of the heavens and earth and seas and stars be if we gave him our best parts? I used to give him my last breath as I was on my way to sleep. That was my time with God, my last conscious thoughts as I was fading. And as Mr. Wonderful can attest to, once my head hits that pillow, you have about thirty seconds until I'm out.

That is what I was giving the one who gave it all for me? I started thinking about leftovers and how surely the God I serve deserved more than just my leftover tired minutes at the end of a long day. What if I turned things around and gave him my best minutes, the ones where I was fresh and his new mercies were already waiting for me along with my steaming hot cup of coffee? What kind of relationship could we have if I let him have my most precious time, the time I usually hoarded miser-style for myself? I justified it for years by saying God would understand. After all, I have all these kids and responsibilities, and I don't have any time to myself. But what if I shared my time with God and gave it to him as an offering of love? What could happen?

I now begin my day superearly. For those of you who know me, you understand this is painful on my part as I am not a morning person. But that's part of my sacrifice. I start early and alone with my Jesus and my coffee. It is quiet and dark, and the house is sleeping, along with all of our occupants. There isn't the usual buzz of activity and frenzy that will happen in a couple of hours. It is simply me and Jesus, some coffee, and a sunrise. I read my devotions and quiet myself so my heart can hear and so I can know what he would have me do for the day.

Now, every day, I look forward to our time together, even if it's much earlier than I would like to be awake. Every day I am rewarded by a renewal of my heart and my mind and my will to do my best for my family on this day. No matter how wrong things may go later or where I end up—the principal's office or stuck in traffic, both of which are distinct possibilities some days—I started my day on the right note. And that note is like music stuck in my head the rest of the day, setting the tone and tempo for where I go and what I do and how I love on my family.

Whatever the situation—whether it's with my kids at the dinner table, Mr. Wonderful on date night, or my Jesus in the early mornings—when I give more than just my leftovers, it never fails that I get even more in return.

Last, First

It's official. We are done having babies. Unless, by some miracle, the snippage didn't work on Mr. Wonderful, we are out of the baby-making business. If I think about this too long, it makes me a little sad. I probably shouldn't be; I have my hands full with four kids. Every day is an adventure, a leap of faith, a test of sanity. I guess by the time you get to four, though, you figure, what's one more?

Some of what makes my heart weep is the realization that all of Baby Houdini's firsts are the last firsts we will see in our children. The last first time someone crawled. The last first time we heard a baby say *mama* or start to walk or give us slobbery, wet openmouthed kisses. These last firsts are going by too fast already, and I'm just trying to hold on.

Appreciating those firsts this time around is what I'm trying to do. It's going to be a while until I get to be someone's granny. At least it better be. These firsts will have to live in my memory for years until the next generation of babies comes along. I don't know if I can handle that. Some days I'm still kind of surprised to find myself with a kid in diapers at this point in my life. When I drop off Baby Houdini at mom's day out, I have to suppress my fear that middle schoolers are now becoming moms. When did I become a "mature" mom?

After this last foray into parenthood, I thought our family would feel final, like we had completed the stage of baby-having and were graduating into the baby-raising portion of our lives. But I haven't heard *Pomp and Circumstance* playing in the background yet. I'm not wearing any kind of motherhood graduation cap and gown. Somehow, and please don't tell Mr. Wonderful this, our family doesn't feel complete yet. It still feels like we're missing someone. Notice I didn't say *something*.

We started certification to become foster parents right before life completely fell apart a couple of years ago. Mr. Wonderful and I felt the pull on our heartstrings that there were too many kids in foster care without enough quality foster parents. We filled out the forms, did an initial application, completed nine or ten hours of training. And then our lives cratered, so everything that didn't involve eating, sleeping, keeping our children safe, and keeping Mr. Wonderful alive had to go not even on the back burner but boxed up and placed in the attic to be taken out at another point far in the future.

The place that we currently occupy may not be where we want to be yet, but we're not where we were, which sure feels good. We are coming out of a bad dream, a nightmare; and though things are still a little foggy, we are awake. I am so grateful not to feel scared and worried and sad and awful all the time that it makes me think, Will we be able to foster at some point? Would we be able to complete the training and do the hard thing that we felt God was calling us to do a few years back? Was it just a call to obedience and we weren't supposed to finish? Or did our detour happen but now we're getting back on track so we can fulfill our commitment?

I don't have the answers to this yet. I wish I did; then I would know if I have more firsts coming. God broke my heart a long time ago for the orphans of the world. There was no sudden realization that I needed to adopt babies. It wasn't given to me in a dream or burning bush or flash of lightning. I just always *knew* I was supposed to. I've broached the subject with Mr. Wonderful—real, casual-like, saying things like, "Hey, how would you feel about adopting?" He looks at me like I suddenly grew a rhinoceros horn straight out of my forehead and starts hyperventilating, so I'm pretty sure he hasn't felt this tug in his heart. Yet.

At one point in a recent discussion, the same one where Mr. Wonderful thought I had gone clinically insane, he asked, "Haven't you done enough yet?"

I thought about that for a moment. He had a valid point. We have two adopted boys and two biological kids, and I never can remember which is which. But then my heart felt the ache of every child who doesn't have a forever family, the tears of babies who just need someone to hold them and hug them when they fall down, kiss their scrapes, and read them bedtime stories. Someone to tell them they are loved and show them in small everyday ways that they are worthy of love. And my heart broke wide open all over again for all the world's forgotten, abused, neglected, and unwanted. I haven't done enough until every child has a safe place to rest his head, a grown-up who will comfort him when he's sad, a forever family to call his own. None of us have done enough.

I don't believe this is just my calling. Right now, if you don't know about the plight of orphans everywhere, if you haven't heard yet that there are half a million orphaned children in the world by conservative estimates, you may be able to turn a blind eye. For a while. But this is quickly becoming an everyone problem. When we have kids growing up in our broken foster care systems who age out and have never experienced the love of a family or the security of being wanted and needed within a family community, they may not know how to sustain a relationship. They may not understand how to stay out of jail or away from drugs or that getting pregnant when you are practically a baby yourself is a hard way to do this life.

Maybe you are not called to adopt—that's totally okay. There are still important things you can do for the least of these. You can pray. You can raise up foster parents in your church or take a meal to that coworker who just adopted a baby. You can donate your time or your money to worthy agencies that are in the trenches trying to match up kids with parents. You can talk about it, start conversations or thoughtful discussions about it.

Maybe Mr. Wonderful and I are truly at capacity with four kids. Some days I will admit I feel like there's more than four. Four seems like at least seven, makes me wonder what seven would feel like. Don't worry, babe, I'm not saying we should have seven kids. I know the thought of that would make you grab your inhaler and stick your head between your knees. But I do feel like, perhaps, just maybe, there is the outside possibility that there is one more kid-shaped space in our family that hasn't been filled. If this is the direction we are headed, I believe God will do the necessary work on my sweet husband's heart and mind, bringing us further down the path of healing and restoration than we are now. And if it's not, then he will do the work on mine.

I get that the reality of adding another child, both in time and chaos, would not be easy. If anything, at the beginning, we would all be transitioning and trying to shuffle around into our new places and roles as big and little brothers and sisters, all while showing God's love to yet another little one. It would probably be a little painful. Transitions usually are. This would be an act of pure obedience on our part. I think sometimes we have this idea in our heads that blessing means comfort. I'm not sure this is always accurate. Sometimes blessings are so uncomfortable that we don't even see them as blessings at the time.

Mr. Wonderful is a big enough man (literally) to anchor my crazy. So when I talked to him about this potential kid-sized space that may still be available in our family and asked him to pray with me, after he breathed into a paper bag, he agreed to do just that. We don't have our answer yet. We won't be making a move until we do. And in the meantime, I still have all these firsts I get to watch. Big Brother is starting middle school in just a few days, and I am in complete denial that this is happening, even though we got his class schedule and put his books in his locker and toured the school. I just cannot believe that this tiny, scrawny, spiky-haired, old-man-see-through-to-your-soul-eyed baby, whom I'm certain I only picked up about two weeks ago in an airport of all places, is starting a whole new chapter as a middle schooler.

This may come as a shock to you, but I cry at nearly every new chapter, every first that my children enter. My coping mechanism for the whole entering-middle-school thing has been that all summer I ignored the fact that it would be happening. Now that the day is nearly upon us, I feel the letting-go process starting all over again.

Big Brother is on the cusp of teenhood, and all I can do is think about when he was a baby. How a little wisp of a baby came to be mine by flying halfway around the world for twenty-one hours with barely any sleep. The day after I got him, I discovered he was even teenier than I thought because he was wearing multiple layers of clothes. I'm remembering how my sweet toddler "helped" me study in law school by using his little crayons to underline in his books (and sometimes mine) just like he saw mama doing. I read oil-and-gas cases while I fed him his bottle. His bedtime stories were constitutional law.

If he grows up to be a lawyer, it's completely my fault. He would be great at it, though. He is confident without being overbearing, thoughtful and sure of his convictions. I pray this serves him well in middle school.

He is getting ready to start this whole new chapter, and I find it disconcerting. I so vividly remember moments from my own middle school experience that they practically happened yesterday, moments that formed and shaped me for better or for worse. I went to middle school in a much different time. Much less scary. I was there when you didn't worry about someone coming in and shooting up the school.

Although I remember in eighth grade, there was a guy in our class who brought a gun to school. No one was scared. He wasn't threatening anyone with it. I remember all of us standing near his locker looking at it, admiring it, not really thinking about it being a threat to our well-being. He got caught and kicked out of school, and I remember that seemed a little odd since I went to school where every other truck had a gun rack. Living in the Southern part of the United States, guns were just part of our world, but not in the scary way they are today.

And now I'm sending Big Brother off to a much bigger, more cosmopolitan school than I went to. He will attend with a bunch of kids I don't know, whose parents I didn't grow up with, and he will begin striking out on a whole new life—a large chunk of which I won't be privy to unless he tells me or, more accurately with this closemouthed kid, unless I ask *exactly* the right question. I know these changes are necessary unless I suddenly begin homeschooling my kids, and believe me, no one wants that.

I don't like this at all.

I know how fast this time will fly. I stress about having enough time for the extracurriculars that are to come. I'm already encouraging mediocrity among my children since they outnumber licensed drivers two to one. I know I will miss every second of chauffeuring and being pulled seven directions at once when I have a quiet house. Excuse me while I go cry now.

There is quite a dichotomy between the proximity my bookend children are to me. My youngest, Baby Houdini, is still snuggled in as tight as he can be, needing lots of mama time. I often find him underfoot or wrapped around my leg or sitting next to me in my chair. I trip over this kid a lot. Then there's the oldest, Big Brother. He is still tethered fairly tightly to me, but I'm starting to feel some slack, some give in the line. These two precious boys seem to be at opposite ends of the spooling that goes on between a mama and her babies.

I cannot wrap my head around this passage-of-time thing. I get that Big Brother must be in middle school because I now have three other kids behind him. And when I look in the mirror, I appear to be a few minutes older. Hours max. I feel caught in some sort of continuous time warp throughout my life. Didn't I just graduate high school? How am I old enough to be responsible for this many little humans? Where did my twenties go? How have I packed this much life and job change and reinvention and children and love into my life already?

Time continues to pass, and I continue to hang on, remembering that these kids are only in my care for a short time. When Big Brother starts sixth grade, I will only have six more years to cram all the life lessons, memories, fun times, and serious milestones in before he leaves the nest to pursue his own life. I will only have six more years with all of my babies permanently in my home and my care. That doesn't seem like enough time.

That's why I hold on so tightly, I suppose. Why I'm making such a big deal about all the last firsts. God has blessed me with four babies from all over. If he chooses our family to be blessed with more, I'm ready. If not, then I know he has something else in store for us, some other way to help the orphans of the world. For now, I will continue to pray for babies without homes, and I will enjoy each time someone asks me about adoption. I love to talk about how blessed I am. And all the while, I will keep careful watch for all these last firsts, appreciating them and storing them away until there are new ones.

Late

Here is a glimpse into a rough day for the Traveling Circus. We all wake up when the doorbell rings because the electrician whom we forgot was coming is already here to repair the wiring for the incessantly chirping smoke detector, which kept me up most of the night. I finally fell asleep but then slept through my alarm. Because of the abrupt wake-up, Mr. Wonderful starts on the wrong side of the Mad Cow, seriously cranky and having forgotten that he was going to be in charge of getting the Littles to school because I have a site visit in another town.

The Littles are thrown off by Mr. Wonderful's outburst about the same time that the fifth grader informs me I'm supposed to go see the assistant principal about an incident involving a bloody nose, which means I have to call the ex about said incident. Baby Houdini has not only climbed out of his crib but also, during his escape, has had a wardrobe malfunction of the grossest kind. His diaper couldn't take his acrobatics, and now there are multiple places that need a good steam cleaning.

Little Sister has an issue with her shoes, yelling at the top of her lungs, "I DON'T WANT TO WEAR THESE SHOES! THEY AREN'T TIGHT!" No one responds because we have no idea what she means. Ironically, it's Little Brother, ADHD safely tucked away somewhere, who seems to have it all together on this day. This is proof that we woke up in some kind of alternate universe.

And I'm out of gas, literally running on fumes of fumes. Both me and the car.

These are the days when my prayers are of the "please help me not to crush my children and use my driving words in front of them" variety. And please give me guidance when I talk to the principal at the school, the new school where we've only been for a couple of months, and now I've already been to the principal's office with both older boys. Oh, and, Lord, please give me insight at my site visit, safety for my children, and help being a good wife to Mr. Wonderful, whose Mad Cow has been a pain in my keister this morning. Sweet baby Jesus, please help me to love on these children you've blessed us with, to be there for them, to have their backs, and to make them own up to their mistakes. Please, God, just take this day and my heart and keep it safe and protected and make it new because, otherwise, I'm just going back to bed.

And, while we're at it, thank you for some peace and quiet on my drive, and for some good girlfriends I will be venting to about this disaster of a morning. Thank you that this car in front of me is finally going the speed limit so I might make it to my site visit on time. Thank you for warm sunshine, leaves falling from the trees, and only a minor and periodic north wind bringing the cold with it. Thank you that even though my skirt was tucked into my tights, I managed to fix it as I exited my car, so I'm pretty sure not too many people saw my underpants. Amen.

All by 8:30 a.m., folks.

I don't know how people without Jesus survive days like this. I'm barely making it with him. I don't know how, if you don't have someone bigger and better than yourself to believe in, you could survive all the mudslinging and slopping that life seems to do. There are days where my life seems so out of control that I barely recognize it as mine. On those days, I keep reminding myself that out of chaos comes joy and blissful moments if you are willing to look for them in the midst of the crazy.

Working and having these four munchkins around and being a caregiver for Mr. Wonderful with the Mad Cow makes me an official CME: chaos management expert. When we have additional kids over at our house, I almost don't notice. They seem to come in as a herd, graze in my pantry, and then leave in a mess of noise and boy funk. If your kids come to my house, they will probably be put to work as part of the group alongside my own children, picking up after themselves, unloading dishwashers, helping clean up after dinner. This is the only way to keep the mayhem at bay. You're welcome.

Being a CME just means that I am probably juggling eleventy-seven things at a time—and dropping some of those things, some days, lots of those things. But I'm trying. As the self-appointed mayor of Crazy Town, I just have to keep going. Maybe on days like this, we eat cereal for dinner. I believe eating cereal for dinner just shows the world we don't take ourselves too seriously. Days like this are when I keep finding pencils with the erasers chewed off. I don't ask, and I'm not searching too hard for the culprit. Of course, this will be the day that I find a trail of red mud through the kitchen. After I just did my annual mopping. Oh, red mud, why must you vex me so! This is said with a shaking fist because Mr. Wonderful's size 15s are impressive methods of distribution for the stuff.

All of this to say that now I have some pretty decent reasons for being late.

Through the years, I've been late for tons of stuff: graduations (my own), weddings (also my own), appointments, meetings, lunches, dinners. I'm nondiscriminatory in my lateness. It doesn't matter what type of event it is or how long I've known the person I'm meeting; I will probably be two minutes late. Maybe as many as ten. I try not to be super late; in fact, contrary to my family's belief system, I try not to be late at all.

I'm just a packer. There tends to be so much on my plate that has to get done because of the Traveling Circus and the Mad Cow. The fact that I'm still trying to hold it together for the Wegener Foundation while doing this writing and speaking thing seems to be pushing my boundaries of time. The concept of time is one of those fluid things for me: it doesn't feel like it has sharp, definite edges.

Mr. Wonderful calls this my time warp. I get in it, and suddenly twenty minutes turned into two hours, and now I'm scurrying around to make sure everybody is doing whatever they're supposed to be doing. We're all running late. This is infinitely frustrating to the men in my life. It started with my dad; then we added Mr. Wonderful. Now Big Brother shares that same look of simultaneous wonder, frustration, and confusion. Like, how do you manage to do that?

My dad's motto when I was growing up was, "If you're early, you're on time. If you're on time, you're late." He never got to the part about what happens if you're late. Probably a good thing. Apparently, Dad, Mr. Wonderful, and Big Brother are all on the same page with this. Me, not even the same book.

Late sometimes gets a bad rap, but it isn't always a bad thing. I've been late a couple of times in my life, the kind of late where it's time to take a pregnancy test. That worked out pretty well, despite the lateness of my childbearing years. When I thought I was too late to have babies, late worked out for the best.

Our late is often God's on time.

Here's some incredibly awesome news if you think you're too late for something: with God, it's never too late. Your story isn't finished yet. It is never too late to come back or start over or begin something new or finish what you started. It is never too late to answer God's call. I don't care if you are four or fourteen, forty or eighty—God has a plan for you. A specific dream that he put in your heart, not by accident but *completely on purpose*. Maybe you haven't thought about that dream in years; but under the dust and the debris and all those suitcases full of your past baggage, there are the remnants of the seeds of the dreams God put in you that only you can accomplish.

Don't ever think that you've reached the end of your story.

I recently discovered a great group called Project Semicolon. People get semicolons tattooed on their wrists or ankles or keep a drawing of a semicolon somewhere nearby. The semicolon acts as a reminder that their story is not finished because, sometimes, where we would choose to put a period to end the story, God chooses to put a semicolon; the story isn't over yet.

It is never too late to begin telling your story, living your God-given dream and destiny, answering the call. Don't worry if you are a late bloomer. Lots of us are. God uses us late bloomers just like he uses everyone else who seems quicker on the uptake. Look at the Bible story of Abraham and Sarah, forefather and mother of a great nation of leaders and kings. One word for you: *elderly*. Like, so old had this happened in the present day, they probably would have been living in a nursing home when they were having babies, assisted living at the very least. This brings me comfort as I'm just trying to stay out of reading glasses while I still have a kid in diapers. With

Abraham and Sarah, even at their advanced age, God was just getting started.

That's great for biblical times, you might be saying, but what about now? Did you know Picasso painted into his nineties? Or that President Reagan was receiving Medicare when he was running our country? Now, that guy was a real grown-up. Mother Teresa, though she was always Mother Teresa-ing, didn't receive worldwide recognition or the Nobel Peace Prize until she was almost seventy. She could have retired and been driving an RV around to see the world. Sometimes overnight success is years in the making. Don't think that because suddenly hasn't happened for you, it's not on the way. God's timing is different from ours.

Don't imagine for one minute that you no longer have something to offer the world or that your story is finished or that you are destined to live out the rest of your days as you have been. Keep going, keep pushing, keep talking and telling. Keep living and experiencing and thinking and dreaming and growing so that you can keep telling your story because you are the only one who can. God didn't give your dream to someone else by accident. He knew what he was doing when he chose to give your particular dream specifically to you. He didn't make a mistake, even if it seems too big and bold and scary. If he has called you to it, he will lead you through it.

Being brave and bold doesn't come naturally to me. It is God in me, convincing me that even with all my faults and failures, my lateness, my baggage, and my chaos, he is using me to accomplish something for his glory, for his kingdom. I may not get it right the first time, or even the twelfth; but with God in me, if I keep my eyes on him, I can't miss. I won't be late.

My story isn't over. Neither, my friend, is yours.

Shift

In these last few days before summer ends and we start school again, I find myself longing to freeze where we are right this moment. There has just been something magical about this summer. Oh, we're still in the middle of the insanity, dealing with Mad Cow, fighting the VA for everything my soldier deserves, figuring out how to make ends meet now that Mr. Wonderful has retired. But I think the magic has come from the gratitude that we are no longer where we used to be.

Perspective has a way of pointing you toward good. Two summers ago, our world was literally falling apart before my very eyes. I was pregnant and tired of running all around town with a net trying to catch my husband and make sure he didn't kill himself or someone else. I was trying to stay pregnant despite my early contractions and trying to protect my other children from seeing the daddy of our house coming undone. There are no instructions for this. Some days I did all that I needed to do poorly. Or not at all.

Last summer, we had just survived moving with four kids under ten. Twice. We were getting settled, but Mr. Wonderful's medical retirement was still up in the air. We were trying to prepare for it, but there are no instructions for this either. In the best of circumstances, retirement is a glorious moment—the culmination of years of hard work celebrated with parties, cake, going-away promises to keep in touch. The reality of our situation was that a medical retirement when Mr. Wonderful was thirty-five and we still had four kids from diapers to elementary age to feed, clothe, and support was more a major life stressor than celebration. Mr. Wonderful loved being an army guy; he wasn't ready for retirement. It was all he had known for fifteen years and had expected to know for fifteen more.

This summer, though life is not perfect by any stretch, I feel more settled in my soul. More gratitude. More room to breathe. It's like the atmosphere around me has shifted. I look at my children and want them to stay *right here*. The ages they are and the space they occupy is really beautiful to me right now. The sibling love and caring makes me so happy. They still fight, playground-justice-style, but they are quicker to forgive, to find resolution.

Yesterday at speech therapy was a prize day for Little Brother. We go every week, but prize day only happens once in a while. He got so excited he went into silent mode. Being overcome with excitement is the only time, besides sleeping, that silent mode ever happens. He did something that just made my heart physically squeeze with love. Have you ever had a heart so full and soggy it just mushed? This was my heart yesterday. Instead of picking a prize for himself, which he so deserved for all of his hard work, he saw a fairy doll his Little Sister would love, so he picked that instead.

Oh, my heart.

This is the same kid who recently told me, "Mama, I think the only thing I really need in my life is Jesus' love."

This. This right here.

When Little Brother is not fighting his mind and body for control, his heart is so soft toward others. He picks up on feelings and changes in the air around him. I've not known many kids his age, or even grown-ups really, who have his compassion. Little Brother often has to war himself because of the ADHD—we work on paying attention, listening when other things are going on, sensory issues, balance, fine motor skills. These are things the world and his school and grown-ups tell him he needs to do to get by. Secretly I wonder if maybe he is more right than we are. At seven, he already came to the conclusion that Jesus' love is it. All we need. All she wrote. Some people never get this, chasing jobs or money or people or fame or time or the trappings of a treadmill. We tell him he needs to learn our way of doing things. Maybe he's already got it, and the rest of us need to learn from his perspective.

This kid is the one who sometimes has uncontrolled outbursts of sound and motion. It's like his spirit is just too big for the little body it currently inhabits, so it has to come out, squeezing past his lips or bounding out through his cartwheeling feet. He can't sit still or be quiet. At times, this makes us cah-razy. But then he says or does something that shows his oversized heart, and I just have to squeeze him tighter as I learn from him.

All the way home from speech therapy, he was outbursting with excitement to give Little Sister her fairy doll. We were driving Mr. Wonderful's truck, and let me just say that a truck cab is a small, confined space that acoustically multiplies sound. Little Brother was so joyful at just the thought of how excited Little Sister would be at the sight of this three-inch fairy doll, probably purchased at a dollar store, that he could barely contain himself. The truck cab could barely contain him.

When we got home, the exchange was so sweet I wanted to capture it in my heart forever. It was just a miniscule moment in our day, but it's a memory that I will take out often and run my fingers over like a faded and worn quilt when I'm an old woman and my children have moved on to their own lives. Little Sister's eyes lit up. They both went into silent mode and started dancing, joy exploding from their little bodies in too much emotion to stand still. And then she showed him his Batman car that she had somehow fixed while we were gone. He had been heartbroken about it when we left, and she had spent the afternoon working on it so her brother wouldn't be so sad. That's when the cartwheels and break dancing were busted out.

These little moments, slices of our lives—these are the times I am holding on to with all my might. These are the memories that will serve me well in my old age.

This summer has been full of these times: eating popsicles after swimming at the neighborhood pool all day, juices baptizing each kid in sticky summer sweetness; the baby snuggling in with me when he's sleepy sweet but doesn't want to go to bed yet because he just needs a little more mama time; going across the street to my neighbor's house to share a love of caffeine and crafting; redoing furniture with Mr. Wonderful, bringing new life to pieces long forgotten and discarded; watching the sun rise from my dining-room window after some coffee and Jesus time; enjoying moments of writing as my fingers tap the keys of my computer; Baby Houdini running to the living-room window to watch a train while loudly yelling, "Choo chooooooooooooo!"; watching Big Brother morph into this middle school–ready kid—new glasses, new haircut, new smells, and new tallness that I'm not yet ready for; seeing Little Sister ride her bike in our driveway with her party-on-top sparkly pink tutu and business-on-bottom tennis shoes, ever practical in her footwear choices.

I have a feeling that these moments have been here all along. I'm pretty sure what has changed, what has shifted, was me—my heart, my attitude, my gratitude. Sometimes, when you are in the middle of the mess, you cannot see through it. All you can see is the mess, and you are just trying to find your way out. But when you get a little perspective, you begin to look around, look up, change the way you view your world.

A shift occurs when we are able to find those celebration moments in the middle of the middle. Even though life may be falling apart all around you, even if you don't have the answers yet or you're still sad or you wish things were different, what would happen if you allow your perspective to be shifted? What if you started viewing your life, not as if things were falling apart but as if the pieces of the puzzle were being lovingly put into their places? This is messy at first: you only have some corner pieces and edges done. The only picture you have is the one on the box, and the box is missing. But then things start to come together. Bigger and bigger chunks of the puzzle are put in place, and suddenly things start to take shape. To become recognizable. The same but new.

Our summer, the one I want to freeze us all in for the foreseeable future, hasn't been without worry or problems. This summer is probably one of the most stressful we have had: figuring out how to bring in extra money to support our family, finding more therapies for Mr. Wonderful to try as there is no one right PTSD therapy, going to extra doctor's appointments and filling out extra paperwork as we try to finish the retirement process with the VA, finding out that Little Brother needs two hours of therapies himself every week, squeezing in work around the very limited childcare we are trying to afford, going to book signings and speaking at any event that will have me since God has given me a story to tell. More of this than I would like pulls me out of my comfy pants.

Looking at it from my to-do list seems daunting. Switching the view of what I see, having a ta-da list instead, shifts the attitude of my heart and changes the perspective of my soul. This helps me realize that even a few steps away from the middle of the muck where everything seems to be falling apart is a good place to be. We are not where we were two summers ago when I was terrified that I would lose both my baby and my husband. We have moved past the newness of the Mad Cow and traumatic brain injury diagnoses and the barely-hanging-on sobriety of last summer.

And maybe we aren't making progress by leaps or jumps or even visible markers every day, or every month. But with the passage of weeks and months, I can see that we are making progress by degrees. That is still forward progress.

I am learning not to hurry through situations on my way to the space I have deemed important. Slowly I am seeing that the state of my world around me is where celebration lies if I seek it out. Growing, changing, shifting—these are a part of the journey that should be celebrated and embraced as new friends. This is where appreciation for the distance traveled comes, where celebration for the battles already behind us lies, where gratitude for the journey God has placed us on lives.

The middle of the middle. Take a few steps away, and there is more clarity. More genuine joy at having survived. More love in the offering of self. More stretch and give in time. There is a fluid nature to enjoyment of the space. Give yourself some breathing room.

Shift yourself. Your space. Your heart, mind, and soul. And prepare yourself to find joy in the shifting of the atmosphere around you.

Hooah

Facing Giants

Status update: feeling aggravated. We walked in the door, and before I even had time to put my keys in the bowl and the diaper bag on the hook, Baby Houdini had broken a lightbulb, partially emptied a bookshelf, and spilled some milk. I kid you not. He's like the Tasmanian Devil: he moves fast and in a whirl of dust and wind and destruction.

I may be too old for this.

He is trying to keep up with his three older siblings. This is bittersweet. Here I am, trying to enjoy every moment of his babyhood as it may be our last, and this kid is trying to accelerate it by doing everything early. The only reason he didn't crawl early was because I wouldn't put him down. I couldn't help it. That wittle face makes me want to talk all squishy and squeeze those pwecious cheeks of his. As for walking, it's not like I pushed him down *every* time he stood up.

I was in such a hurry with Big Brother. I couldn't wait for the next everything with him. My first time experiencing everything as a mom made me so excited. I now see the folly of that thinking, so I'm trying like heck to stop time, or at least slow it down even as Baby Houdini chases his siblings just trying to be part of the gang. They are all so sweet with him, often slowing down what they are doing to show him how. We have stairs in our house that I didn't want him to climb up until he was three. So, of course, at twelve months, his brothers are patiently teaching him how to climb up. Opening doorknobs, a skill I desperately hoped we would save for much, much later—well, his sister demonstrated how this worked. I would put those childproof doorknob thingies on, but then Mr. Wonderful and I would *never* leave the house because we would be trapped. They should really call those adult-proof.

Baby Houdini loves to wear his daddy's shoes. He doesn't seem to be bothered by the fact that he has to slide his feet when he wears them. Shuffling along in his daddy's dress shoes or tennies, this baby has some skills at walking in shoes ten times too big for his feet. He's so happy and proud of himself. He's not daunted by the fact that those are some really big shoes to fill. He will grow into them long before I'm ready for him to.

Mr. Wonderful and I have been on a growth extravaganza ourselves the last two years as well. We have stared death in the eye, and death looked away first. That sort of changes how you react to living. We (mostly) don't have freak-out moments over the little things anymore. Little Sister throwing a tantrum over her shoes every morning—no freaking out here. Some sighs and eye rolling, yes. But no freaking out. Three e-mails and phone calls from Little Brother's teacher in the first two days of school? We got this. Now we try save our freaking-out for the Herculean issues we've had shoved in our faces over the last few years: sobriety, the Mad Cow, its subsequent treatments, depression, panic attacks, continued healing after I nearly lost Mr. Wonderful, and fighting with the Veteran's Administration about everything.

These are some giants.

I'm not talking manageable issues here. This is definitely David-and-Goliath territory. We are most decidedly in over our heads. Any one of these is enough to break us, and when you combine them all, even with Mr. Wonderful's big shoulders to carry a portion of this load, it is all too much. Too heavy. So exhausting. And it's not like we can just tackle one of these things at a time to make it all less daunting. We have to handle it all. At once. All of the time.

We just can't do it.

By our own human strength, we cannot face these giants. If it were up to me, I wouldn't even get out of bed, knowing that they were all waiting for me. Every one of them has the power to knock us out before we even throw the first punch. If I had my way, we never would have gotten in the ring with them in the first place. I'm a lover, not a fighter. This is Mr. Wonderful's territory. He's the specially trained army guy who made a career out of warrior-ing. I'm a hippy mama-lawyer-musician with no battle training, unless you count kickboxing. Give me a good beat and call it a dance fight, and I'm there. I'm not afraid to go all *West Side Story* on you.

Ma-reeeyah.

These giants have knocked me smooth out, but I keep getting back up. Not by my own strength, though. We're quickly approaching the two-year anniversary of the day I found Mr. Wonderful in the kids' tree house, which was also the day he took his last drink. I would be lying if I said this didn't give me pause—or, more realistically, stop me in my tracks completely. Last year, I dreaded the whole month of September. It was only a year past nearly losing Mr. Wonderful, and it just didn't feel far enough away for me to be comfortable. At the end of August, the very approach of the month itself made me feel panicky and weak and scared and traumatized all over again. I had watched him fall apart slowly throughout 2013, and in September of that year, everything just sped up. Like we were on a train for a leisurely jaunt and then we gradually sped up to the point where we were going too fast to make the upcoming curve. Then I saw the conductor bail out. I knew things were going to end badly.

September.

Even now, I don't like the taste of this word in my mouth. Two years ago, September contained all of my fear and worry. All of my nightmares coming true happened in September. Now it seems when it comes around again, I feel myself holding on to my people more tightly. I was scared I was going to lose both Baby Houdini and Mr. Wonderful two Septembers ago, and I almost did. So I squeeze them more, hug them more, kiss all my children, and snuggle with them more in September.

The Mad Cow is no joke. I have asked our countless doctors how Mr. Wonderful got so far down the road after his deployment before it really kicked in. I guess thirty days off and three counseling appointments postdeployment aren't nearly enough. The military way, though it's not written in any of their field manuals, is to soldier on. Self-medicate with alcohol if necessary as that is the acceptable method of soldiering on. Deployment is a time of brotherhood that isn't experienced anywhere else, which winds and intertwines the best times of one's life so tightly with the worst times that it creates a difficulty in treatment. The best and worst can't easily be separated.

Combine all of this, let some time go by, maybe throw in a couple of childhood situations or traumatic events, and you have the perfect recipe for the Mad Cow to rear its ugly head years after the event. Mr. Wonderful's deployment was not long after 9/11. Our doctors told us that, on average, it takes a veteran about ten years to seek help for his or her PTSD. Usually, it's because life has gotten so unbearable for the veteran that if there is still a spouse or loved one or family member who has stuck around, the only option left that keeps the veteran alive is for them to get treatment. Enter Meredith at about year eight post-deployment, and there you go. When I came onto the scene, Mr. Wonderful was still able to cope, to soldier on. There weren't any warning signs or red flags that any of this was coming. He still had a few good years in him before life would begin to unwind.

Something you may not know about Mr. Wonderful is that he has been on his own since he was about fourteen. You read that correctly. I'm talking about the kind of "on your own" where you drop out of school because you need to work to provide yourself food and shelter. The kind of "on your own" where you couch surf with friends until you can't. And then you sleep in the parking lot of a Circle K for a while until you find someplace a little more homey. The kind of "on your own" where you have no one to guide you, bad decisions are followed by worse, and jail or early death is likely. That is a whole other chapter maybe I will write about someday, but suffice it to say, God and the military saved Mr. Wonderful. That is why he wanted to soldier on, to do the job he loved, and continue putting food on the table for his family by serving his country forever. That is why he didn't need anyone or anything. He was used to figuring it out on his own.

September.

Last year in September, we knew his medical retirement was coming. We knew we weren't going to be able to survive financially on it. We also knew he wasn't going to be able to work a civilian job for any amount of money in the world. We began fighting his severe depression on leaving the job he had loved, the only one he had ever known for fifteen years at the same time we were fighting the Veteran's Administration for the benefits they promised when he enlisted for this gig.

The VA was created to help veterans, especially those wounded after wars and times of deployment. Sounds great, sign us up! The original intent of the VA was honorable; but now, speaking from experience, it's a bureaucratic, labyrinthine nightmare when you try to seek help, medical care, or services. The building itself, the wait times for appointments, the paperwork—dear Lord in heaven, the paperwork! We have a small file cabinet and three boxes of paperwork that it has taken to get Mr. Wonderful medically retired and his rating appealed. Three boxes.

Dear Veterans Administration, this is not okay.

And just so we're perfectly clear, VA, going to your facility shouldn't be a trigger for someone with the Mad Cow, throwing them into panic attacks and making our days more difficult than they need to be. And yet it is. You finally schedule us for an appointment, but when we show up fifteen minutes before our appointment time as requested, we have to wait an hour and fifteen minutes for our actual appointment. Then we're told we need to go visit two other places within your facility for goodness-knows-what where we're going to have to wait again and that we can't even find because they have moved since the last time we were there. Going to the VA is an all-day affair, one that I can assure you neither Mr. Wonderful nor I look forward to.

As a friend of ours says, if you're not angry when you go to the VA, you will be when you leave, #truth.

And even though the copious amounts of doctors that Mr. Wonderful has been seeing for over three years have said my guy is not going to be able to do a civvie job, y'all at the VA with your incomprehensible math and complicated rating system refused to give him more than a 90 percent VA rating that would make sure he was able to fully medically retire. That extra 10 percent would make a huge difference to our family. I bet you weren't expecting a fight from us on that 10 percent.

Well, guess what. I have on my kickboxing dance shoes.

We've already covered this hippy mama-lawyer-musician's mad researching skillz. So while we have been fighting the VA and trying to walk the path of sobriety every day and keeping the depression at bay—all while raising children—I continuously research treatment after treatment for my soldier. And not just traditional treatments that the VA recognizes and provides. I'm not so sure I trust you guys to do what's best for my veteran. I'm pretty sure I saw some vets from the Civil War era wandering your halls the last time I was there. I jest, but the wait for treatment is nearly that ridiculous.

One of the best therapies we have found for the Mad Cow is Mr. Wonderful's service dog. We worked with a great foundation called TADSAW (Train a Dog, Save a Warrior) that has helped us with training. Charlie the service dog has become his dogly guardian angel. She isn't even fully trained yet—Mr. Wonderful and Charlie will continue to train every week until she is fully certified—but the amount of peace that she has helped usher into our home has been remarkable. The kids understand that when she's wearing her vest, she's working for daddy. But when she's not, Charlie is our family dog who fits in our family like she was ours all along.

We are still facing these giants every day. I look back to two Septembers ago, and it makes me a little jittery. But then I see where we are now, and with the benefit of hindsight, I can see the distance we have traveled. I can also see that we weren't alone when we were traveling it. The whole one-set-of-footprints thing? I get that now. Because it wasn't my kickboxing dance moves or Mr. Wonderful's warrior strength that got us here.

It was straight up Jesus carrying us.

All those times two Septembers ago, when I was wearing out my knees, begging God to save us, wondering if he could get to us in time before that speeding train crashed or derailed, he was carrying us, and *I didn't even realize it.* We were already in the palm of his hand. He was already doing his part, but we couldn't see it. At times I couldn't feel it. Even when I was hopeless and alone and didn't know what to do, he was already carrying me while carrying out his plan to save my family.

As I look back to two Septembers ago, I can see now what I couldn't then. He had surrounded me with people to love on me and help take care of our family while Mr.

Wonderful was getting the treatment he needed. He allowed our lives to crumble past the point of us being able to rebuild by ourselves so that we would rely squarely on him to fix us from the inside out. Mr. Wonderful had to sink to the very bottom, to be threatened with losing everything and everyone he loved, so that he would accept the help and the treatment he needed. How else do you get a guy who has been on his own since fourteen to give up control and give in to the One who holds our very destinies in his hand?

God wanted a sober spiritual leader for our home and a hurting man to get help before he further hurt himself or his family. He wanted a wife to learn to lean on her Daddy harder than on her husband, and he wanted children to see their parents failing on their own but succeeding in the hands of the Creator of all.

We don't believe in coincidence around here. Everything that happened, even the bad that I thought we couldn't live through or survive or find a way to put behind us, was necessary to bring us to the point of complete surrender—of our ways, of our wills. And when we surrendered, we found that God's way for us was going to be exceedingly abundantly better than the way that we had for ourselves.

September.

As it approaches, I am starting to turn and shift and realize that September is not a month to be feared or dreaded or hurried through. No, it is a month to be celebrated. For within that month is the anniversary of sobriety, healing, new beginnings, a new marriage, and a reminder that every day is a day to be cherished. September is no longer my enemy but my friend. September is the month that turned every part of my life inside out and turned my eyes and my will to my best friend, who saved me and my family in ways no one else could.

Welcome, September.

Waiting Room

I got cut off in traffic today. This tiny little car swooped in front of my giant Suburban; and for one moment, while using my driving words, I actually considered running it over. Don't worry, the kids weren't in the vehicle. The wheels on the bus would've been going round and round so I wouldn't have had time to think this through as clearly if they were. My 'Burb was twice this car's size, so I just about monster-trucked it.

And then I saw a sticker hanging from the rearview mirror. It was a handicap sticker, and the car was driven by a little lady so small she could barely see over the steering wheel. And she was at least one hundred and seven. So then, I felt a giant amount of guilt wash over me for wanting to crush her like a bug. Ironically, it was a VW Beetle. I'll just let that sink in.

We all seem to be in such a hurry these days. Everything is instant and 24-7 and available and happening right now. We want our food fast and our driving faster and our texts returned immediately. We want high-speed computers and movies on demand. There is instant messenger and instant coffee, neither of which I really like. Drive-throughs stay open late or twenty-four hours. We want our streaming and downloading and tweeting and posting to happen right this minute. If I think about all of this too long, it just makes me tired and a little short of breath.

Sure, when I'm running late with four kids who have to be dropped off in seven places, I hurry. With the amount of caffeine I usually have coursing through my bloodstream on a daily basis, I tend to go warp speed by the time I'm on my third cup. My rule is if my heart's not racing, I haven't had enough. I'll freely admit I have been known to break the sound barrier when a school calls and says one of my kids is sick or hurt.

Big Brother, the little old man who is quickly morphing into a bigger little old man, is my kid who gets the award for ending up in the emergency room the most. He has had stitches, dislocated his elbow twice in two weeks, and broken both bones of his arm, also twice. This last time, I knew it was really bad when I went to pick him up from his school, and his arm was bent. Like, his arm was smiling at me bent. It is truly an out-of-body experience when you are helping your child to the car and trying to remain calm while his arm is moving like Jell-O. On the outside, I was saying soothing words and moving with purpose and confidence. On the inside, I was *freaking out completely*, screaming at the top of my lungs and running around in circles, waving my hands in the air like a woman gone mad.

When we got to the emergency room, it was an especially busy day, even for our little hometown hospital, so we had to wait for them to check out his Jell-O-y seemingly boneless arm. This kid was so tough. He teared up when he first saw me at the school, but not one tear after that. Barely any moaning or fussing. Just trying to hold his arm in a way that wasn't as awful as all the other ways.

That is a helpless feeling right there. Watching your baby suffer and not being able to do one thing about it. Not being able to hurry the staff along at the ER no matter how I tried, not being able to make him more comfortable, not being able to kiss away his boo-boo. All my running around and caffeine and super-mom-here-to-save-the-day flitting about couldn't do anything to take away his pain. Time seemed to pass so slowly. I would have sworn to you, we were in the waiting room for at least three hours, but I'm sure it was only about fifteen minutes. Waiting was painful; I needed some instant gratification that day for my boy.

Unless you're waiting for a baby to be born, not a lot of great stuff happens in the waiting rooms of hospitals. The people we saw in the waiting room were in various stages of disrepair: there was a woman who was green and vomitus, a man who had cut himself badly and was dripping red stuff everywhere, and a woman who was having major breathing issues.

Who got to go in first? Breathing wins out every time.

We are all about the instant, the now, the immediate. We want everything when *we* want it. That doesn't leave a lot of room for savoring, or change, or growth. There are times in life for all of us that we find ourselves in a waiting room of sorts. And usually, much like hospital waiting rooms, it's not somewhere we would choose to be.

I currently find myself in a waiting room: multiple areas needing triage, all competing for top billing on which will be treated first. My typical way through this used to be railing against it like a small spoiled child in pain: "Let me outta here! I need to see a doctor RIIIIIGHT NOW!" But of course, in that waiting room, Jesus is working on things and on me and is doing it all in his perfect order. I want him to heal Mr. Wonderful yesterday and show me how to do this speaking and writing thing better and fix Little Brother's auditory processing and ADHD—this second. But often, his timing isn't about right this second.

Being a child of God has never been more relatable to me than since I became a parent of a near middle schooler. Those changes—hormonally, physically, mentally, and emotionally—come fast and on top of one another, making life much more interesting. I kind of thought we had already reached our max capacity for interesting around here. Now with Big Brother going through so many changes at once, it seems he knows pretty much everything. He forgets his place as a kid in this house, trying to boss his siblings or even me at times. This is the kid who used to put himself in time-out when he was about three. He would march his little self into the time-out spot before I would even have a chance to put him there. He knew when he had gotten just a little too out of bounds and would parent himself.

I forget my place sometimes too. I forget that the waiting room isn't a place where you start bossing God and running around trying to make things happen. This room is a place for rest, reflection, learning a thing or two, and maybe some gratitude. Definitely some gratitude. Sometimes I get so caught up in trying to do my part that I end up trying to take on God's part. I'm finally figuring out that my responsibility is to submit my will, my life, my time, my family, my everything to him. His is to give me his words, his way, his destiny for me so that I may become a conduit and vessel for carrying out his plans. This doesn't relieve me of my responsibilities; it simply defines and clarifies. And it takes the pressure off.

Sometimes in the waiting room, the pain gets intense. Your spirit hurts. Your heart is broken. You can no longer function as the person you once were. And as you're seemingly waiting for God to get around to your problems, your wounds, the wait seems interminable. You wonder what in the world could he be doing while you're hurting so bad? What is taking him so long?

What we don't see from our puny human vantage point is that God is doing his part. He started it before we got to the waiting room, long before we even got hurt. His ways are indeed higher than our ways, and to be in the waiting room is hard. But if we understand the goodness of God, maybe at some point in the future, we might understand that this room will have served a higher purpose than our own.

Maybe we're not even in the waiting room for ourselves. I have found myself in situations I didn't understand only to look back later and realize that my time in the waiting room was really about how he was going to use me and some particular skills he had placed inside me for the benefit of someone else.

Waiting rooms and the moments spent inside of them can go one of two ways. We can focus on the pain, the hurt, and the wound itself. We can rail against the system, wondering why we aren't being treated already, yelling and whooping and hollering about how unfair it is that we haven't been seen yet. We can allow our wounds to take center stage, letting them grow and fester and turn us into piles of regret or unforgiveness or bitterness.

Or we can use our time in the waiting room. There is a purpose if only we will quiet our bellyaching to take a look around. Are you there to learn? Does God have something better for you than what you've been waiting on? Can you stop holding on so tight to your hurt that someone can even get close enough to you to take a look?

The truth of the waiting room is that there is a purpose to pain. There is a reason, maybe not visible or understandable to you at this very moment, why you are there. And if you use your time wisely in the waiting room—growing, learning, trusting God that it is no accident you are there—your insides will start to change even before everything around you shows signs of recovery.

Can you trust God enough to let him work on you through the pain? Even if it gets worse before it gets better? Can you believe the truth that he is faithful?

You are not alone in this waiting room; I am right there with you. We may have different wounds, but you can trust that he is already at work. And he will not stop until his good work in us is finished.

Say Yes

We have instituted a rule at our house that no one talks to mama until she's had her first cup of coffee, which means I hear whispered conversations from the kitchen that go something like this:

Big Brother: Did she have her coffee yet?

Little Brother: I can't tell. You go look.

Big Brother: No, you. I looked yesterday.

I'm not proud of the fact that I often start the day swinging and thrashing about. The kids don't want to get swatted away like gnats, so they tend to keep their distance at first. In my defense, it's in their defense. If I'm not quite awake and haven't become fully caffeinated, there's no accounting for my actions. Or my thrashing.

My redheaded she-child has a tendency to try to wake me up just by staring at me creepily in the middle of the night. Tell me you wouldn't wake up swinging if you felt a pair of eyes boring into you, willing you to wake up.

This is why I now start my day much earlier than my children. It gives me a chance to get my coffee on, write, spend time in conversation with Jesus without us being interrupted because, hey, I'm talking to the Creator of the universe here! Can we get a little privacy? I now attempt to begin my day with some gratitude for the gorgeous sunrise or the sweet sounds of the baby playing in his crib, trying like the dickens to wake his brother up, who could sleep through an air-raid siren.

Starting my day with coffee, Jesus, gratitude—I'm finding that this is the way I need to do things so that my answer is yes. Otherwise, it's not just no but hell no. And that's just inappropriate when you have little kids in the house.

Saying yes.

It's not always our first reaction, especially as a parent. Can I stick this metal object in this plug-in? Can I try skydiving? What would happen if I drive Daddy's truck? Do you think I can climb that tree to the very top? Can I get an iPhone? Do you have any money? Can I have a sleepover with these kids we don't know whom I just met?

Saying no has been my go-to. It's my natural reaction to both kid questions and life. Should I write a book? Should I talk about our crazy? Should I tell our story, the one I wish was someone else's? For a while, saying no has been a defense mechanism so my mind and heart and soul could realign to my new paradigm. It's really weird when things shift: if you're not paying attention—and sometimes even if you are—one day you will just wake up and have the realization that things are radically different, as if the universe was transformed while you were sleeping. You wake up, and your surroundings have become unfamiliar. Life isn't just different; you're not even sure it's your life anymore.

At various points in my life, I've been so busy trying to live and breathe and take care of my responsibilities that I wasn't paying close attention. I could see things were changing bit by bit, but not in an alarming way. And slowly my world morphed into something new and different. Those changes are much less jarring than waking and finding life as I knew it was gone, changed, rearranged. I've had a few jolting changes like that, where I looked around and didn't even recognize the terrain. This is disconcerting. Absolutely wild, unforeseeable changes happened in my life without my knowledge. Here's a news flash for you: we're not in control—of other people, of the twists and turns life can take, sometimes not even of our own circumstances.

Learning to say yes again after the tectonic plates have shifted under you and carved out new bumps and ridges or mountains and valleys is daunting. No is the defense. Yes opens up the door to only God knows what. What if we don't like the yes? Then we won't have anyone else to blame but ourselves because we will be the ones who opened the door.

Saying yes.

It's a leap. It's a rush. Yes is a door opener, friend maker, adventure beginner. Yes can be a conversation starter, a forgiveness giver, a reconciliation maker. This is why yes is so scary. It turns someday into today. And while someday is comfortable, like those pants you put on as soon as you get home after work (or that you stay in all day because you work from home, just saying), today requires immediate action.

Someday thinking gets you down the road with your dreams. Someday I will…

Go to college.

Ask him out.

Call my mom.

Say I'm sorry.

Someday I will chase my dream, forgive her, work out, change jobs. Someday feels full of potential without all the responsibility of today. Someday is excitement without effort, joy without pain, achievement without work. I have been guilty of someday thinking. I'll write a book when the kids are out of the house…someday. I'll start working out when I have more time…someday. I will get organized… someday. It feels great to think about someday, like a soft, comfy blanket to wrap ourselves in when we want to imagine our life or situation or finances or relationships or status or jobs are a different way.

Someday is lovely, like a dream we don't want to wake from. Today is reality, but someday is possibility. Potential. The problem with someday thinking is that we put all the potential into the future instead of the day before us, which means we do nothing about today except dream of our someday.

We are so arrogant. We live as if we have an unlimited number of somedays, because we always have another someday—until we don't. At some point, for each of us, the somedays end. And do you want to get to today only to realize it was your last someday?

Dreams are good. Thinking of a better life, a better way, a different pace or style or theme for how you live is good, great even. But when we get stuck in the someday thinking, we miss all the awesomeness of today because we are focused on someday. Today is the day that we can do something about. Today is the day we can make a change, take a step, move forward, even if it's not the way you imagined or pictured today going.

Saying yes is the way to change your someday thinking into *today doing*. Think today thoughts: Today I will start on my dream. Today I will take a tiny baby step toward reconciliation. Today I will open a door, start a conversation, fill out paperwork, research my options, join a gym, take a walk, get to know my neighbors, go to church, forgive my parents, talk to my sibling, find a new job, foster a child.

Today I will say yes.

This is hard, and more than a little scary. Today doing invites the unknown. You will meet opposition. You will have stumbling blocks. You won't feel as warm and fuzzy about today doing as you did about someday thinking. You will be tempted to give up, give in, walk away. And why not? All the cool kids are doing it.

I speak from experience when I say it probably would be easier if you did give up. Why do people stay in jobs they hate? Why do people not speak to their loved ones for thirty years because of something no one remembers? Why don't people live out their passions? Because it is hard.

Excuses are plentiful and, well, excused. They are acceptable reasons to live the status quo. Status quo is just a fancy way of saying standing still, not moving, remaining the same—all while enjoying your someday thinking. I've not only lived someday thinking; I have relished it. I have burrowed deep within it. I got so entrenched in it that I made a sweet little space for myself there, hanging up posters and getting a comfy chair and bringing in good snacks. I had a nice spot to enjoy my someday thinking.

Except.

I realized I wasn't serving any purpose. I wasn't fulfilling my destiny or serving my God with my someday thinking. Jesus was a man of action. He didn't just talk; he did. He served. He washed feet. He preached. He fellowshipped. He forgave. He celebrated. He rose from the dead.

His miraculous rising is our call to action, our invitation to not be comfortable with the status quo. Hear me now and believe me later: Most days, I'd rather do my day job, hang out with Mr. Wonderful and my kids, wear my comfy pants, and forget I have a story to tell. I would really rather bury it deep in a box and drive it out to the desert and never have to see it or talk about it or write about it ever again. Our story is hard and gross and ugly.

But that's not what I'm called to do because Jesus makes our story beautiful. He turns our ugliness into a gorgeous tale of redemption. I'm not supposed to sit on my derriere and dream about telling our story…someday. I'm supposed to be out, telling it wherever I can, to whomever will listen, asking God to be with me and give me the right words and the write words so that I can do what he has asked of me. I am to tell our story, painful as it is, so that others will know they aren't alone and so that God's glory can be seen for miles around our family.

Today is happening right now. Today requires action. Today means saying yes. Someday becomes today when we say yes and start doing. We don't have infinite somedays. Someday our somedays will run out. Where do you want to be when that happens? Do you want to be wishing for more somedays, or do you want to be down the road today?

Someday thinking. Today doing.

Our choice.

Brave

Do you remember that clumsy phase in about junior high where your feet grew so fast it threw off your equilibrium entirely to the point you were constantly bumping into things or tripping over your own feet? Our oldest, Big Brother, seems to have entered this era of body morphing. I hear him ricocheting off the walls and furniture all around our house. He seems surprised that he's no longer in control of his body.

Just wait until you're forty, man.

Baby Houdini is on the opposite end of the learning curve. He is just learning to walk around; and though he is brand-new at this, he feels the need to try to run everywhere, even though he can't stop very well yet, or turn corners on a dime. Between the two of them pinballing through our house, I now have scuffed walls, and it often sounds a lot like a herd of something has been loosed.

The two kids in the middle aren't less loud or destructive, even though they are pretty adept at movement and haven't gotten any big growth spurts yet. Little Brother bounds from place to place superhero-style, practicing his flying skills and leaps while Little Sister dances, skips, and hops behind him.

It is really loud here, and I have very few breakables left.

When our kids fall down, which seems to be so excessive I'm thinking of having their inner ears checked, I always say the same thing: "You're okay. You are strong and brave, so you will be just fine." Maybe since they fall down a lot, they will hear this affirmation so often over the course of their lives that they will start to internalize it. Then when they do the metaphorical falling down as we are all apt to do—the failing, the disasters, the wrong turns, or wrong people they will surely encounter—they will remember what I've always said to them:

"You're okay. You are strong and brave, so you will be just fine."

I hope that convinces them to get up, no matter how many times these fallings and failings happen. The older I get, the more I realize how valuable failing is, how important it is for things to not go well sometimes. When I look at the situations and moments and times and relationships that I have considered successful, I realize that nearly all have come *after* I have fallen, or failed miserably, or stumbled, or gotten knocked over. Many of my best parts of life have come after I have completely messed up.

How does that even happen?

How can you fall down and then find success? By getting up, dusting yourself off, and trying again, from what I can see. Lots of successful people started with failure: college dropouts, written-off students, quitters, losers, cheaters, liars, adulterers, murderers. The Bible is full of those types.

Look at David, a man after God's own heart, who not only adultered with his neighbor but went one step further and had her husband killed. Or Moses, who killed a guy, stuttered, and then led an entire nation to the Promised Land. Or Jesus's tribe of mismatched followers who ran the gamut from fishermen to tax collectors to stinky dead guys. You can't tell me there wasn't some soap-opera drama in that bunch.

If there are complete screwups who somehow found the courage to try again, to keep trying until they were able to reach their goal, then that means we can too. That means we're not limited to our failures or our screwups or our colossal misjudgments of money or time or people or resources or our own abilities. This is so exciting! This means there's still hope.

What is the difference between a current loser and a former one? In my humble opinion, it's the act of getting up, learning from mistakes, being brave enough to try again, to keep going no matter what.

The more modern world is full of examples of this as well. Abe Lincoln was defeated in multiple elections, Steve Jobs was fired from his own company, Steve Wozniak dropped out of college, Dr. Seuss got turned down by a bazillion publishers. Donald Trump has even filed for bankruptcy, four times. People lose all the time. Greatness is often preceded by failure. Mistakes can lead to success, to a better way of doing things.

Being brave doesn't mean you won't fail. It doesn't mean you won't mess up. It is not a remedy against fear. Brave people can still be scared people. They are most definitely scarred people. But the difference is that brave people feel the fear and *do it anyway*. That gives the rest of us hope.

Look at my own Mr. Wonderful. He could have stayed down after the Mad Cow diagnosis. Many do. The tormenting thoughts and nightmares that he bravely fights on a daily basis are enough to make some turn their backs on God or family or healing or, in some cases, on living. The Mad Cow is a rut in his brain that makes him relive scary and terrible things over and over. It causes him to feel guilty about surviving and anger about thriving.

But every day, especially on the hardest of days, he continues to get back up again. He keeps trying, moving forward. If one thing doesn't work, we try another. And he remembers that he's okay. He is strong and brave, and he will be just fine.

Whatever that thing is for you, it is still possible. In fact, it's probable. You're not too old or too young. You don't have too little experience or too much baggage—if you get back up, if you dust yourself off, if you keep going, no matter how you feel or if you're scared or if someone else has told you many times that you're not good enough or smart enough or have enough to get the job done. Their opinion doesn't matter. Yours does. And our Heavenly Father's does.

By the way, he thinks you're amazing.

This may be difficult to believe if you haven't been told anything but complete garbage about yourself. But please let me tell you about this Daddy who wants you to know how special you are, how strong and brave you are. He cares about every detail of your life, every thought in your mind, every emotion in your heart. He has caught each tear you have cried. He numbered your days and the hair on your head and knows your fears, your strengths, your weaknesses. He longs for you to know what he knows about you.

You are special.

There is no other way to put it. You are a unique, one-of-a-kind creation with your own fingerprints, exact eye color, DNA, beating heart, and swirl of emotional puzzles no one else in the universe ever has had or ever will possess. There has never been another like you, and there never will be. You were created for something special. You were made to accomplish your God-given destiny, and if you don't, you will leave a you-sized hole in the universe. If you don't get up after you fall down or mess up, something is left undone, unfinished, incomplete. And that is a real tragedy.

Mistakes and failures happen. And some of them are *bad.* Some of them are fall-flat-on-your-face, leave-you-bloody-and-broken, call-911-then-your-mama mistakes. Sometimes they're caused by you, sometimes by circumstance, sometimes by others you let in only for them to turn around and beat you up with your failures and your shortcomings when you least expect it.

Here is a beautiful truth:

You can't be too far gone. You can't be so burned beyond recognition, so ugly and scarred inside that your Heavenly Father won't want you, won't still think you are beautiful, won't be encouraging you to finish whatever work he has set out before you. He wants you to look in the mirror and see what he sees: a work of art.

What if you are only one mistake away from what you were born to do?

What if that failure that has you questioning if you should even bother getting out of bed today is the one that becomes one of the greatest turnaround stories the world has ever heard?

What if you are so close to this turnaround that if you were just to reach out your hand beyond where you are lying broken on the floor, you would find help and a hand to raise you up, elevating you to a higher place than you have ever been or ever dreamed of your entire life?

What if Mr. Wonderful had not come out of that tree house?

What if he hadn't gone to treatment, or if we had quit on each other?

I write about mistakes and failures because we have lived them. We are able to tell you from our personal experiences how bad failure can sting but to get up anyway because God is not finished with any of us yet. Or our stories.

This isn't a line I'm feeding you. This is the power of the Jesus I serve. This is the man who walked the earth as one of us, who left all that was beautiful and perfect in heaven to come down and live among the mess of us. He is the one who has the job for you. And he is the one who will train you for it.

Even if it looks too scary or too hard or flat out impossible, even if it is way above your pay grade or expertise or comfort level, none of that really matters, I'm finding. You can go to college perpetually or attend the School of Hard Knocks; neither will prepare you for the job the Master has called you to do.

The bad news is that what he is calling you to do probably *is* too hard for you or it *is* way above your pay grade and expertise. The good news is he doesn't ask you to do this job alone.

Whatever God has called you to, he will equip you for. This is the God who makes the impossible possible. We can't do the job he asks us to do by ourselves. What would be the point? The whole "God will never give you more than you can handle" thing—I call bullcrap. Why would we ever need him, turn to him, rely on him if we could handle it ourselves? Relying on ourselves requires no faith. Being asked to do something big and scary with no real resources after you've messed up a time or two, now that's something that will test our faith, increase our faith, grow our faith.

Personally, the last few years of our lives have been about God asking me to walk to the edge—of time, of responsibilities, of life and death, of insanity. I keep getting asked to take a step without being able to see where the foothold is. Kind of like the classic *Indiana Jones* movie where Indy takes a step off a cliff, and only once he's taken a step into seemingly nothingness will the steps actually appear across the chasm.

That's what my life feels like to me now. And as much as I love change and leaping and new beginnings, this constant being-pulled-so-far-out-of-my-comfort-zone-that-I'm-no-longer-in-the-same-country-as-my-zip-code thing is hard. Doing what God has called me to do is hard. Being brave is *hard*.

I'm convinced we all have much work to do in this world. There is beauty to create, books to write, photos to take, encouragement to give, wrongs to right, injustice to conquer, orphans to foster, businesses to start, loved ones to reconcile with. There are big jobs and little jobs and hard tasks and easy items to cross off our lists. But it can't happen unless you get up, unless you try again, unless you remind yourself:

You're okay. You are strong and brave, so you will be just fine.

American Idol

Fifty-seven times a hour, I am interrupted. Most of the time, it's when I am *thinking*. The interruption comes at the critical point when I am gathering my thoughts in preparation for a task or for speaking in a conversation or for directing the multiple players in our little circus. This may come as a surprise to many of you, but I do not just blurt out every thought that comes into my head; no one has time for that. Trust me, that's just too many words.

Interruption now causes my brain to completely melt down. Whatever it was that I was getting ready to do or say will either 1) be completely forgotten or 2) uhm, I already forgot what two was since I just had another interruption. Are you kidding me? Where was I? Oh yes, 2) will come out completely wrong, backward, or upside down. I might use the wrong name or say the wrong word or get to the end of the sentence and lose a word. Apparently, I have the Mad Cow too.

It's disappointing to be this age and already have these issues. I find myself so distracted these days. I am so pulled in multiple directions at once that sometimes I feel like I might just come apart. This is one of the reasons I sing. All the time. Sometimes I'm singing to make myself feel better. Sometimes it's for fun. Sometimes it is to embarrass my children. But most of the time, it is how I stay on task. I am actually singing about what I am supposed to be doing.

Weird, I know. I'm over it. Singing is mandatory in the circus lifestyle that I lead. I need reinforcement and focus wherever I can get it. The world as I know it would end without coffee and singing. Or I would be doing twenty-five to life somewhere, and trust me, orange is not my color. Warning: coffee tangent coming. My love for coffee runs deep. I *love* coffee so much. I *need* coffee so much. If I could, I would marry coffee.

Just kidding, Mr. Wonderful. You know you're my soul mate.

I'm going to admit a former little guilty pleasure to you: I used to watch *American Idol.* I stopped watching when I found out I was *too old* to audition. What, more mature people can't become overnight sensations? We might have dreams too. Sudden success often gets the credit for working hard toward a goal your whole life, and those of us who are putting in the time year after year get this.

....

Sidebar: At some point recently, when I wasn't looking, I became a ma'am. *I was so busy changing diapers that it just sort of snuck up on me. I would swear to you that I'm in my twenties, twenty-nine tops. I know* ma'am *is a polite Southern thing. I have used it myself, and I now teach my children to use it. But I am telling you, I do not wish to be called* ma'am. *Ever. You have been warned, and if you are in the food service industry, your tip will reflect your usage of this offensive language.*

....

American Idol sucked me in like nobody's business because it was about 1) singing and 2) plucking unknowns from nowhere and turning them into the musical flavor of the moment. Some have even become bona fide stars. Look at Carrie Underwood, one of my homegirls from rural Oklahoma who manages to be both an amazing singer/songwriter and person. She makes me proud. She hasn't strayed from how she was raised to go all Hollywood. She gives back, she's a great role model, and she is a heck of a singer.

She is also focused. Just wait until you have four kids and you're trying to write a song, Carrie Underwood!

The distractions around here are everywhere. I have kids with their antics and apparently a word limit that each child must hit per day. Then there's Netflix. Oh, how Mr. Wonderful and I enjoy some binge watching of Netflix. We don't even watch regular television anymore. We watch seasons of shows. Throw in phone calls, e-mails, text messages, iPads, Twitter, Instagram, Facebook, and all the other technologies that have just become focus-shredders and time-sucks for me, and I am in deep, people. I will just get started typing or working, and if it's not a kid banging his trombone case down the stairs at 6:15 a.m., waking up the other three who are going to invade my writing time (this actually just happened by the way), then it's my phone dinging different ways to both annoy the crap out of me and let me know that something is happening.

In our twenty-first-century technology-laden world, is it any wonder I suffer from *distractionism*? This is the inability to focus on one thing at a time. As a woman, I already suffer from this since moms are called to wear multiple hats at all times. My name is Meredith, and I am a multitasker. I am constantly doing a minimum of three things at once, and probably not very well. I often multitask myself into a corner. Working on Wegener Foundation while checking my e-mail while watching a toddler is a recipe for said toddler to end up covered in expensive eye cream—which, of course, I now need as I don't get as much sleep as I should and people keep calling me *ma'am*. If I would have been doing one thing at a time, the baby probably wouldn't be covered in lotion. (Is anyone else hearing, "It rubs the lotion on its skin"? No? Just me then.)

Is there any room in this world so frenetically loud with distractions for a quiet Jesus? This man from a time when life moved slower. Back in Jesus' day, people walked or rode donkeys or horses. If you wanted to talk to someone, you actually had to go to their house, knock on their door, and see if they were home. Since there was no e-mail, to send a message, you had to find someone going to the town where your friend lived, tell them the message, hope they remembered it by the time they got there, and actually found your person and delivered it.

Life then was about waiting. Life now is about hurrying, packing your schedule, being productive. Life seems to have sped up since I was a kid. Back in my day (I usually say this in an old-man voice who, for some reason, doesn't have his teeth in), we walked to school, we played until dusk, we ate dinner together at a table at six almost every night. The weekends were long, stretched-out things where we might have sleepovers. We would definitely go to church. We would finish our homework Sunday night with plenty of time to watch a little television or play some Atari. Yes, we had an Atari; and yes, I was the tricounty champion of Pac-Man. All right, just a trisibling champion. So what?

In the glorious summers of my youth, my family often helped my grandparents who owned a farm. During harvest, our family, and sometimes my uncle's family, would come to my grandparents' little farmhouse outside the rural town where my parents grew up, and everyone would be put to work. The grown-ups all drove wheat trucks or combines, and the kids stayed back at the farmhouse to "help" my Grandma Lodema make enough food for the army of workers. *Lodema* was her real name. She's the only one with that name I have ever known, and that seems fitting. She was a one-of-a-kind lady.

Grandma Dema was a fantastic down-home Southern cook. The woman used ingredients like real butter and freshly butchered meat from their farm. We all couldn't wait until the next holiday or birthday celebration because that meant we would be going to Grandma Dema's. She was such a wonderful and prolific cook that she had a separate table *just for the desserts*. Every countertop and table in that small farmhouse would be weighted down with everything from fried okra and homemade mac and cheese to fresh baked ham, mashed tators, and green beans. She made homemade rolls and often had homemade sand plum jelly to slather on them.

My mouth just started watering.

She showed her family love through her cooking, and she probably could have had her own restaurant or jelly line. But she chose to be of service to her family year after year. She worked incredibly hard in that little hot kitchen all day long, preparing all the meals for everyone working in the fields. She cooked all morning to make lunch; then we would drive out to whatever field everyone was working in to deliver it. Afterward we would go back to the farmhouse and clean up lunch so we could start the process all over again.

Sometimes I would ride in the decrepit blue wheat truck my mom drove. We would wait in the field for the combine to get full; then it would come over and dump all the precious wheat into the back of the truck. We would make the journey, slowly and steadily, into town. I remember that old truck was so rickety that you could see the red dirt roads passing beneath our feet because part of the floorboards had rotted away. Not even missing floorboards would keep us from delivering the wheat to the grain elevator. We would get our wheat weighed, dump our truck, and head back out to the field to get another load. For two or so weeks during harvest, we would do this, as quickly and efficiently as possible before it rained or hailed or something ate the crop or before prices dropped. Sometimes the grown-ups worked late into the night if a storm was brewing. We would watch the lights of the lonely combines scraping the fields out the windows of the farmhouse, where we were much too excited to sleep.

Before bed, my Grandma Dema would make me and my cousins our version of coffee: mostly hot milk, a dash of actual coffee, and lots of sugar. This may be why we were too excited to sleep. We would be laughing and giggling and playing despite all the work going on around us. We knew my Grandpa Clyde had everything under control. He was one of those men you just trusted in any situation because he always got the job done. He was a highly capable man who managed to run a profitable farm most years in Oklahoma. If you know anything about farming around here, you know how impossible of a task that often is. He grew wheat and raised livestock and eventually leased out land for oil wells. He was smart and frugal and a hard-praying man—all prerequisites to the farming life.

He and my Grandma Dema set the example for our family that we would attend church unless we were dead, we would give at least 10 percent of whatever God blessed us with, and we would pray. We would have as many Sunday meals and celebrations together as possible, and we would always have one another's backs. My Uncle Jerry had three kids who were close in age to me and my siblings, so we all grew up like brothers and sisters instead of cousins. I credit my grandma and grandpa for this because they instilled in us, at every turn, the importance of family and how you just show up for one another. Harvesttime was an example of this. Family dropped everything to help out family. Period.

I've been feeling so nostalgic lately. I miss these great people who provided such strong shoulders for me and my family to stand on. Grandma and grandpa came to every band concert and basketball game they could. All four of my grandparents were friends before my mom and dad got married, so the four of them used to do things together without all of us. I didn't know that was unusual; I just thought that's how everyone's family was. At holidays and family events, all of my grandparents were there, bringing my entire family together. This is a very special way to grow up.

And my cousins, even though we're now spread across the country, these are still my brothers and sisters. These grown-ups with lives of their own are still keepers of many of my childhood memories—gathering in my grandma's teeny farmhouse kitchen, circling up to say the blessing, diving into all the good food we had been smelling Grandma Dema making for hours. We played outside, running all over the farm as far as we felt like going, smelling the newly tilled soil, watching every glorious sunset turn into first dusk then darkness so we could catch lightning bugs. Using my grandma's shed as our playhouse, we would mash up flowers to make "perfume" then beg Grandma to drive us into town so we could sell it to her friends. By the way, our perfume container of choice was a prescription pill bottle, and her friends were kind enough to pay us for that awful stink we sold them. My cousin Lee and I thought we were on our way to a family business. We probably owe these ladies a refund.

Simply put, my childhood consisted of family time, outside time, and church time—sometimes all three at once. This was a beautiful and simple life, one I often long for now that I'm caught up in a fast-paced, no-holds-barred, gotta-get-to-everything time. I long for simplicity for my children as well, a time where technology and testing and expectations and preparing for college and their future doesn't need to start by second grade. Where they can just be kids for a little bit.

My children do seem to suffer from all the distraction this world has to offer. As much as I would like to, I can't ban them from all technology—even their homework requires it. Little Brother already has to do math homework on the computer now. That sentence blows my mind. I suffer from wanting to make my kids live under a rock yet simultaneously be able to use technology and keep up with other kids. All these distractions and busyness that multiply and get heavier each year are really convincing me that we need to take a step back—as a family, as a community, as a culture.

Now, busyness equals productiveness, and productiveness equals worth. You just don't hear in a mom's group or around the water cooler at work how someone sat on their front porch and watched the sunset while their kids ran around aimlessly outside. That's not news. How busy your kids are with after-school activities, how high their grades are, how many sleepovers they can have and attend, how many sports and instruments they can play, how many languages they can speak—these are all the ways that we are supposed measure our children and ourselves as parents.

But I just can't.

First, at our house, kids outnumber us two to one, so the logistics are pretty complicated if we're going to have lots of activity doing that requires them to be driven somewhere, which is further complicated by the fact that we live in the middle of nowhere. Oh, and sometimes the Mad Cow means I am the only grown-up that can leave the house.

Second, I just don't want to.

What I want to do is unplug my children and go back to family time, outside time, and church time. I know we should already be preparing for college with Big Brother—I've seen the commercials—but I want him to be fully engaged in his upcoming sixth grade year, not worried about something that isn't happening for six more years. There's a lot of life to be lived in between now and then, and I want him to live it. I want to limit distractions and safeguard my children from the dangers of them.

Getting too distracted from the life we are supposed to be leading is dangerous. Our focus is supposed to be on Jesus, but with his quiet presence and his nonintrusive way, I worry that he isn't loud enough to be heard in this world. He won't shove it down your throat. His way requires silence and stillness so we can hear him over the sounds of ringtones and notifications and binge watching and iPads and social media. Can you imagine Jesus' Facebook page? Relationship status: single. Worked at: saving the world. All his Instagram pics would show him and his disciple homies just tearing it up around the Sea of Galilee. He probably would have had a lot of followers. A lot of haters too.

I guess instead of dreaming about being the next American Idol, which I'm too old for anyway—and besides, this is their last season, so the joke's really on them—I'm going to shut off, unplug, take time, unschedule, savor. I will live a leaner life, putting my heart and my time and my family back into the moments that draw us closer to God rather than toward the noise and distraction that get so loud I can't hear what he has to say.

I want to hear him speak.
I need to feel his presence.
I'm trying to be a woman chasing after his own heart.

Dangerous

I just now realized something.

I have been in a blissful parenting bubble with all my babies under one roof most of the time. We didn't take an easy path to get any of these children, so I try to enjoy sweet moments—the ones where everyone is sleeping—every chance I get. No matter how good or rotten our day has gone, I go check on our kids every night before I go to sleep. Watching their angelic little faces peacefully dreaming reminds me how much I love these little boogers.

As I was walking down the stairs from checking on them, I had a sudden fear, a terrifying jolt of realization. I have lived through hard things and they will too. They will face people and situations and circumstances I can't yet fathom and won't want them to. I can't protect my children from everything; in fact, there's a lot that I can't protect them from when they are just walking around in the world without me. That led to the realization that this whole walking-around-in-the-world-without-me thing is only going to get worse.

Pardon me while I go breathe into a paper bag.

Okay, after a brief panic attack, I have regrouped.

My Bigs, the two oldest boys, go to their dad's on occasion. No matter how great things go there, I can't control what they're exposed to, whom they hang out with, what they do on the Internet. I don't get to tuck them in and hug their growing boy shoulders and figure out just by feel that they're having a bad day even though they didn't mention it. I'm missing out on whole pieces of their lives, and I hate this.

Even my Littles are growing so fast that I just want to yell at time, *Stop! Please slow down!* I can't grab on to each memory like I want to, and I'm trying to enjoy every millisecond of every day, but I get caught up in the things I'm supposed to do, things that must get done. I want so much to keep my children in these moments for a while before they're grown and gone. There is so much we still need to teach you, to tell you, to build into you.

I'm afraid we won't have enough time.

The last several years of my life have been full of wonderfulness. They have also been full of hurt and fear and turmoil and things that I wish that I hadn't had to go through. It dawns on me that as much as I want to protect my children from this, as much as I would go through it all again just to save them that kind of soul-crushing pain, I can't. I won't be able to.

This is the part where I have to believe in God's plan, to trust in it fully. And believe me, it is one thing to trust it for yourself; it is another entirely to trust it for your children.

Mr. Wonderful and I have had multiple discussions about how sometimes when you're going through things that are meant to break you, if you let God use them for growth, those awful things become the propulsion that send you toward God's plan for you.

You become dangerous.

When you don't crack under the pressure, when you let your stumbling blocks become stepping stones, when you allow the seeds of the dream God planted in you to take root even though there is no sunlight, you are becoming something formidable.

Fierce.

Relentless.

In my former life, I had it pretty easy because I didn't take a lot of risks. I led a safe and charmed life that looked pretty from the outside. But, as I found out, even a safe life isn't safe. Even a safe life can get dumped upside down, turned inside out, made messy and weird and unexpected.

That's why now, though I live quite uncomfortably most of the time, I'm happy. Even when things aren't going my way, when we're approaching what appears to be the edge of yet another cliff, when I wish I could spare myself and my loved ones these heartburns, I remain grateful. All the little scrapes, inconveniences, ruined expectations, and spoiled moments have prepared me, strengthened me. They have made me able to walk through whatever God has for me, able to walk toward his plan for me.

Don't think for one minute that I liked what happened to my Mr. Wonderful and me when we were going through our hard time. Don't imagine that I wasn't crying, screaming, cursing, and calling out to a God, who was seemingly nowhere to be found. Please don't assume that I can weather hard things with grace and efficiency like some kind of unfeeling robot.

Repeat after me (in your robot voice): Life. Is. Hard.

I'm not excited about the prospect of facing more hard things in my future. It's like having a second baby—you know what to expect this time around, which makes it both better and worse. I just know that because of all the mud we've sloshed through, all the obstacles we have overcome, all the hurt and save us Jesus moments we have had over the last few years, I am becoming a force to be reckoned with now. I am like a warrior returned from battle.

Before I left my safe village, I was young, naive, sure of myself in that cocky, yet-to-be-tested way that youth often have. I assumed I was both immune and invincible. I went into battle thinking I would be the same person when I returned. I charged forward not knowing what lay ahead, only to be beaten down my first time out. And then beaten down some more.

But like many young warriors, I was too stubborn to quit. And I learned from each battle and each skirmish how to fight better, smarter; how to survive; how to lean on my faith while leaning in, pressing forward. I learned that to survive anything, I needed my Jesus. And the only surrendering I would be doing, the only white flag I would be waving, would be to him and how he wanted my battles to be fought.

It was in the complete surrender to his way that I found strength. I have fought each battle, some of which I never would have believed I would survive, with a courage that wasn't from me. But it was in me because of the King I was fighting for.

Returning from war, I am admittedly road-weary, tired and older, a little worse for wear. I have new wounds and old scars, and I'm still healing from the fight. I am broken in places, limping at times, old hurts aching when there is a storm or weather change.

But I am still standing.

My family is still together.

My Mr. Wonderful is still alive.

And God has a purpose for all of our pain. He is using it every time I tell our story to bring light and hope to someone who is desperate for them. And my battle wounds are proof to those who would listen to my story that I know of Whom I speak.

So I will continue to live dangerously. This is my ministry.

If we aren't doing life in such a way that we pee our pants just a little—and not because we've had a couple of babies and things work differently now—then maybe we're not doing it right. If our choices and dreams and prayers don't make us feel nervous butterflies if they're actually answered or come true, then maybe they aren't big and bold enough.

If our prayers and ministry and dreams are such that we feel like we are in too deep, we may be on to something. If we don't wake up in the morning and suck our breath in through our teeth at wonder and nervousness at what God may be using us for today, maybe we should rethink things. Maybe we are playing it too safe.

I've lived life as Safety Girl.

It's exactly what it sounds like: safe. It is an existence without danger, without too much worry or trouble or bumps in the road. It is a life that anyone can live because, honestly, it is not that hard.

....

Sidebar: This is not to be confused with one of my dear friends we call Safety Girl. She just keeps us all from doing really stupid things that would up the chances of our children being orphaned. We love and appreciate her for this.

....

Living life as the Safety Girl I'm talking about has kept me wrapped up in a cocoon of warm, comfortable thoughts, prayers, hopes, and dreams, which were mostly about what *I* wanted, what *I* needed, what *I* was going to get out of my day. I was supercozy, and life was good. Why ask for anything else? Why strive for something different than comfortable pants and warm fuzzies?

Most people won't, and I don't blame them. I didn't for the longest time. That's what makes the dangerous life so unique. Not everyone chooses to live it. Not everyone can handle it. Look at Jesus, that rebel with a cause. What did he and his disciples model for us? Jesus wasn't a king adorned with jewels, living in a palace, eating all the food he could fatten himself and his friends up with. He didn't wear silk robes and party with celebs and have the coolest DJ or make it rain denarii or have a golden chariot with twenties. It wasn't all about the shekels.

He walked dusty roads. Constantly.

He wasn't even recognized as himself in his hometown.

He was mistreated, made fun of, tested, scorned, tempted, tortured, wounded, betrayed. He was a wanted man. A criminal. He probably wasn't comfortable. He definitely wasn't cozy.

He was dangerous.

This is the life we're signing up for if we follow that guy. And though it scares me, I'm giving up my comfort to live life dangerously. I'm forgoing keeping my pain hidden where it would be more comfortable. I'm talking about the last few years with everyone I meet when I'd really rather forget they existed. I'm trying to be really real when it would feel so much better to wear my mask and pretend like nothing bad ever happened.

Mr. Wonderful and I are living proof of the miraculous hand of God and his goodness and his mercy and his enduring love. We will share our story with those who aren't quite convinced of his power. We will tell our battle tales around the fire, encouraging others who are in the midst of their own wars. We will show others how to put on armor and take up that uncomfortable, difficult fight. Together we will rise as warriors, and when any of us fall down or are surrounded or can't find our way, we will band together and pick each other up and fight alongside each other. We will continue to learn how to be fierce when it comes to faith and family.

It would be so much easier to be Safety Girl, so much more comfortable. But I've already been there. And I'm not going back because I'm a woman on a warrior's mission: I am here to be Jesus' hope and his love in human form for anyone who needs it.

Make no mistake, I'm a little bit scared. Some days, I'm shaking in my boots.

But I am dangerous.

Shut the Front Door

We have a fly problem in this house. I blame my children. Every time one of them comes in or goes out, it's the same old story: they stand there with the door wide open, letting the outside in and the "bought air" (as my Grandpa used to say) out. *Bought air* is air-conditioning if you didn't get that. He was a clever, clever man.

I'm constantly saying, "Shut the front door!" mostly because the front door is open, sometimes because I'm surprised by something: like that Big Brother's boy funk can hit me in the face as I approach the top of the stairs long before I have entered his room, or that Little Sister can throw a forty-five-minute tantrum over how her shoes have to be "tiiiiiiiiiiiggggghhhter!" (I have to give her credit; she really knows how to commit), or that Little Brother has suddenly forgotten how to eat with a fork.

Because of our open-door issue (not to be confused with our open-door policy—y'all come on over!), I find myself in the kitchen or the bathroom or our bedroom oasis, and all I hear is buzzing. Who let the flies in?

....

Sidebar: If you sing this to the tune of "Who Let the Dogs Out," it's much more fun. Feel free to buzz instead of bark. Is it stuck in your head? My work here is done.

....

I have become the master of the flyswatter. I'm getting pretty good at taking aim at the little suckers. The other day, I got two at once. Please hold your applause.

My kids let flies in and bought air out, and our doors seem to be open or only halfway closed all the time. As I walk through the house, shutting them because suddenly all my kids have disappeared, I see how absolutely disgusting the doors are. Recently, my pantry door seemed to be slathered in peanut butter and a sticky substance I could only assume was honey. The act of touching the handle just about sent me over the edge—it was so gross! As a mama of four, I have seen and touched some "bisgusting" things, but this was at the top of the list. *Bisgusting* is courtesy of Little Sister. She felt the need early on to tell her brothers how yucky they were sometimes.

I feel your pain, girlfriend.

Upon the pantry-door discovery, I immediately went to find the culprit because mama does not equal maid. It is usually pretty easy to narrow down. All I have to do is ask which kid made a PB and honey sandwich and bam! Case closed. Duhn-duhn (this sound effect brought to you by *Law & Order*).

After Little Brother and I cleaned the pantry door, I shut the front door yet again. I was about to blow my top and probably throw a minitantrum when God really spoke to me about something.

The summer before I started sixth grade, we moved to a new house in a new town. I was okay with moving; I wasn't okay with the house we bought. To my eyes, it had ugly yellow trim and was a 1960s ranch-style house with zero personality or nooks and crannies like the older two-story house we were moving from. It had wall-to-wall shag carpeting, and the master bedroom was all red, *floor to ceiling*.

Never mind that a coat of paint would change everything. I was embarrassed by its hideousness.

My bedroom was in a different part of the house than the other bedrooms. My parents' room was down at the end of this long hallway, which was spooky, even in the light of day, because there were no windows or natural light. And at night, fuggedabouddit. There was no way, unless I thought I was actually dying of scabies or rabies or scurvy, that I would go down that hallway toward their room because it was just too scary. It was the kind of pitch-black where you couldn't see where you were going; you had to feel your way. And I was always a little scared of what I might feel if I stuck my hands out in front of me.

I was starting middle school as we moved to the new casa, so there was about to be a whole new series of doors for me, some of which had frightening hallways like the one leading to my parents' bedroom door. Throughout my time here on this planet, I have stood outside many a door. Some were already open, and I could kind of peek through. Others were "bisgusting," and I wasn't sure I even wanted to touch them, much less see what was inside. Still others were fancy doors, luring me in with how beautiful they were. High school and college and marriage and divorce and job changes and remarriage and parenthood—these were all doors I have stood outside of, wondering what was on the other side, thinking about whether or not to go in.

I can't get this sign I saw the other day out of my head. It said, "Praise God in the Hallway!" What a blessed reminder for me, especially as I am standing outside of several unknown doors even as I write this book. Every change in life comes from walking through a new door. Or not. Sometimes we get to the door, and it is too funky or revolting, all covered in peanut butter and baby schmutz and sticky substances we can't identify. We're just not sure we can touch that door, much less walk through it.

Sometimes a door looks really inviting—it's a game-show door. Insert cheesy music and sparkly door decorations here. "What's behind door number 2?" the announcer asks excitedly. Everyone is clapping and cheering and in the excitement of the moment it seems like such a good idea to pick door number 2. This door is gorgeous and has been decoupaged or bedazzled or decorated with balloons and streamers, but when we walk through it, we see that it was all a sham. Disappointment fills our hearts as we find that the door was really a fake door, and all that was waiting behind it was a braying donkey and a bag of hay.

There have been times throughout my life where I have been scared to open a door. The door looked questionable, and since I couldn't see behind it, I was not sure I wanted to open it. There might be failure, or success, or change; and we all know how painful change can be. There have been dark and spooky hallways and areas so tight and narrow and black as night where I couldn't see my hand in front of my face that I needed to walk down just to get to the door. Sometimes the door is locked when you get there, and you knock and knock, but no one seems in a hurry to answer.

I have stood out in hallways of doors probably a hundred times. And whether I'm waiting for God to open the door or whether he has made me capable of opening it myself, that hallway is a hard place to be. Being in the hallway can mean that you're so close to the door you can feel it, but for some reason, it's not time to open it yet. And if the hallway you're in right now seems a little like the hallway to my parents' room—dark and narrow and long and terrifying—you're in good company.

I personally haven't enjoyed most of my hallways like I should have. I have been in too big of a hurry to get to and through the door. All the wandering through the dark, wondering where I was, where is the end, how things will go made me rush through an important part. Being in the middle of the transition, on your way to the door, is where the doubt starts to creep in. Am I heading the right way? Did you hear that? What was that noise? How much farther can that door possibly be? Is this even the right door? How many times have you been in the middle of a transition and you felt yourself paralyzed with fear or indecision? The hallway can be scary. Often they are not well lit.

I am trying to transition my idea of transitions, to change how I view the hallway.

I think it's time to embrace the hallway.

Embracing it means *accepting the place I am in right this minute*, even if I am not crazy about it. I have always said I don't believe in coincidence, and if I hold this to be true, then I must be in the hallway for a reason. There must be something I need to learn or prepare for or experience before I go through the door. The hallway must be someplace important.

Say what?

This whole time, my entire life, I've been racing through hallways, skipping them whenever I could, taking the quickest route to the door I could find. If the hallway looked too frightening, I might avoid it altogether. And now I think it's possible that the hallway is just as important as that door I am racing toward. That hallway, that transition, is a huge part of our life journey, and we need to treat it as such.

How many doors have I missed because I ran through or skipped the hallway entirely? How many joyful moments, silver linings, lessons, or celebrations did I overlook? If I didn't take the hallway because of fear, then I might not have learned the things I needed to that would have prepared me and propelled me forward. That is sad and daunting all at the same time. Here I am, worried about the doors I am trying to bust down, break through, open up, and I am probably not ready for them since I didn't walk through the hallway first.

Shut the front door.

In that hallway, the transition on our journey, we need to be soaking up each and every minute. That whole enjoy-the-journey thing—it starts in the hallway. In our journey through the Mad Cow, I have been running toward the door marked "Healed," but in my hurry, I may have missed out on some of the gifts waiting for me in that hallway.

No matter what your hallway looks like, whether it is creepy with bad lighting and scary music or filled with family pictures, it's time to praise God in the hallway. Wherever you are *right this minute*, whatever space you are occupying right now, whatever door you are headed to, take a moment. Praise God in that hallway and look around. What are you supposed to learn or gather or experience here? That is going to be an important part of your journey.

And, if you don't mind, should you happen to see my kids in that hallway, will you please tell them their mama said to shut the front door!

Cow Tippin'

Epilogue: Scandalous Grace

Please be gentle with us. I have opened wide the door to our crazy.

You have been given a glimpse into the home and hearts of a family who loves, struggles, and lives with the Mad Cow. My hope is that when you peek in the windows of our lives, you see at our core our love for Jesus and one another, the only way we have come through this part of our journey intact. I also hope that it makes you consider the possible journeys of others you meet—everyone is fighting something. Everyone has struggles behind the closed doors of their homes.

From what I have gathered, we seem to be the exception to the rule of military with severe PTSD. The rule that we see played out time and time again is that if you have the Mad Cow, your life will constantly be an untenable mess. If you have managed to keep yourself alive, if you have figured out how *not* to lose yourself in a bottle or pills, then you are one of the lucky ones. It is fairly commonplace that you will have very little family left, few friends, and financial stability will be precarious at best. The Mad Cow is isolating that way. It takes away everything you love. Unless by some miracle you have loved ones who have stuck around long enough to see that you finally get treatment, most everyone who could help usher in healing and help with meds or doctors or remembering appointments or handling your finances is long gone. That leaves the person suffering from this hideous disease to fight their demons entirely alone. Sometimes they don't even know they need to fight; oftentimes they lose their will to fight.

Feel free to drop by any VA Hospital in this country if you need proof.

When you look into our lives, into our home, I hope you see us in all our Mad Cow glory, sitting noisily around our dinner table. Our table isn't fancy, but it is where some of our best moments as a family take place. Also, some of our worst. We are a spicy, loud crowd; and if you ever try to join us for dinner, good luck getting a word in edgewise. Hopefully we won't spill anything on you. And I pray everyone remembers that we don't talk about farts at the table, but I can't make any promises. As often as possible, we sit at our table in the eat-in kitchen for dinner. We pray, sometimes after fighting over who will say the prayer, and then we eat. Then the talking begins.

I learn a lot from these conversations.

For instance, the other night, we were going around the table discussing what we thought our spirit animals might be. This is better than the topic of most disgusting smells but worse than the topic of favorite desserts. Mr. Wonderful was, of course, a lion. He has a lion tattoo on his chest, and it matches his lionheartedness. When we voted on my spirit animal, it was unanimously unicorn. This is not even a real animal, and yet my family agreed it was just right. I'm not sure what to think of this yet. Except that I do and I love it.

Big Brother is a dolphin: highly intelligent, likes to swim, loves his pod of friends. Little Brother is a hyena due to the laughing and loudness and laughing and silliness and laughing. Did I mention his laughing? Baby Houdini is a puppy dog. He has the puppy-dog eyes and he loves to bark and wag his adorable little tail. Also, *puppy dog* is one of the words he can say so that everyone understands him.

And then there's Little Sister. We decided her spirit animal is a honey badger. If you don't know what a honey badger is, YouTube a video immediately. You will simultaneously laugh and be awed and a wee bit scared. This is how we feel while parenting Little Sister. She makes us laugh a lot, and we are also just a little bit frightened of her.

She is intensely right all the time. And sure of herself. And fearless when it comes to going after what she wants. These are going to be such lovely qualities when she's a grown-up navigating the rocky and treacherous waters of life. Right now, though, it sometimes makes me need to pull my hair out.

She and I have some common ground, though. We share a love—wait, an obsession is probably more accurate. We both heart shoes so much that we almost can't stand it. Sometimes we like to go into my closet and just look at my shoes. I know, we're weirdos. I consider it bonding. My dream is that she will someday be my shoe size, and we will double each other's shoe collection. You are going to have to give me a moment.

Okay, I'm back.

As I purged my closet at the end of the year, I gave away several bags of shoes. I may have a serious problem. The cleaning and organizing—things that aren't exactly my skill set—were actually really soul-stirring for me. There is just something about tackling what feels like a huge problem and making it manageable. It is no exaggeration when I tell you that our closet was beyond out of control. I nearly lost the baby in there once. We have this tiny closet, and I share it with a man who wears ginormous clothes. My only issue with the wonderful house we live in is that our master bedroom closet is entirely too small.

Size matters, y'all.

Cleaning out my closet and dealing with my copious amounts of shoes made me reflect on the last few years. They have been so emotionally messy with the whole implosion-of-our-lives thing and moving and rehab and moving that I haven't actually been able to focus on clearing out the clutter in our house or the crap that clouds my mind, or my spirit. There has been so much clotting and clogging up of our very beings that it made us sick. Let's just say the situation got so bad that I'm starting to have a better understanding of how hoarders become hoarders.

As I sat perched on the edge of this brand-new year, I couldn't help but take a quick peek behind me to see all that we have walked through over the last couple of years. We have gone on quite a dramatic journey that I could not have foreseen. If you told me that not only would we stumble through a valley so dark we couldn't see our hands in front of our faces but we would also emerge into a lightness and joy that I did not know was possible, I probably would have called you a liar to your face.

Hindsight is a gift from above, I'm sure of it. This special vision allows us to see in a truer form what has gone behind us without the blinders of the present moment. I feel as if for the first time in over two years, I am taking off my blinders.

I can see that we have been stomped on, cast out, undone, torn apart. We moved and removed. During dark season after dark season, we had trouble finding our way, gaining our footing. Using this hindsight as a tool of some deep introspection while I was knee-deep in closet dehoarderization, I realized that, for several years now, I had been living in fear.

I was waiting for the other shoe to drop.

Life got so tangled and messy and beyond anything I had the skills to cope with that I got scared. And I just stayed there. So many hurtful events and moments were crammed into such a short amount of time that my memory, mind, and heart didn't have time to process them all. And because they all happened so quickly and so painfully, I got stuck in the common thread of those moments—fear.

I was living in fear.

Just typing that sentence makes my heart beat a little faster. When I write about the last few years, it brings up old wounds. A lot of healing has happened, but there are still some scabs and tender spots, a few places where all the hurt hasn't quite gone away. And sometimes hurt produces fear.

Live in fear for a while, and it starts to feel oddly comfortable. That is the terrible deception of fear. You begin to wait for something bad to happen because so much bad has happened. A nasty cycle begins, and somehow you can't get off the fear hamster wheel.

At the heart of the matter was my heart—wounded, broken, and bruised—some days it felt like it was barely beating, like I might be in serious need of a heart transplant because mine hurt so bad in my chest that I couldn't breathe. Maybe if I got a different heart, I would have a different life.

That's what fear does. It seeps in and tangles itself in your arteries. Fear clogs them up, and a sort of plaque begins to form where once you had clean, shiny pathways for pumping healthy blood. The sludge circulates all through your body. Fear distorts circumstances, mangling them and poisoning your mind and heart until you become diseased.

This is exactly where scandalous grace makes its grand entrance.

In the face of fear and hurt and brokenness and open wounds, God's scandalous grace is the salve that heals even the worst injury. This grace that I speak of is now taken as seriously as bacon or coffee at our house. I can speak about it, attest to it, because *I have experienced it firsthand.*

The scandalous grace Jesus poured over me and my family throughout our last chapter is overwhelming. There have been so many grace-full moments that I am at a loss. We survived death beating down our door. We lost the hope and possibility of a new child only to gain a baby boy whose timing was impeccable and whose superpower is Joy with a capital *J*. With one belly giggle or mischievous smile or "big squeeze"—the most sweet version of a baby hug with his tiny arms wrapped around my head—Baby Houdini can change the mood of even the most downtrodden.

We know a little something about being downtrodden.

God's scandalous grace saved Mr. Wonderful, saved our Bacon, saved me. Our family exists only because of it. Without it, the legacy of our family would have withered on the vine. His grace was enough to pull us back from the very gates of hell.

Do you know of anything else that can do that?

I don't. When we were in the midst of 2013, I thought that my pink champagne life was done—finished, emptied, poured out, party over. The trash and broken party favors were littering the floor, and I couldn't imagine that I would have too many reasons to celebrate anymore.

I was so wrong.

....

Sidebar: Mr. Wonderful is probably copying and pasting that sentence even as we speak. I know, babe. You don't hear that too often.

....

This grace I speak of is scandalous because it is given away. It is free to anyone who wants it, and in this world, that is truly something. Nothing of any true value is ever free, and this most priceless gift—unearnable, unmatchable, unimaginable—is.

I can barely fathom it. With that hindsight thing, I can see all the moments where God's scandalous grace existed for me the last few years—the placing of just the right people in our lives, the rebuilding of our marriage and our family, the saving grace that got us on the road from heartbreak to healing, the countless ways that we were shown love and that we were cared for by the body of Christ.

I start this brand-new year no longer living in fear. I now live steeped in gratitude, humbled by second chances, healthy hearts, and new shoes. No matter what comes, I have my history with amazing grace to lean on, to remind me that it does indeed exist. I have seen how God can work everything for our good. I have been a firsthand witness and recipient to good overcoming evil, triumph besting tragedy, life overcoming death for top billing on the five-o'clock news. God has a plan, a destiny, and a way; and though I don't always understand where he is taking us, I know that I trust him with my life. With all our lives.

I no longer have to wait for the other shoe to drop because I have put on my new shoes of peace—both of them. And God has wrapped me in the blanket of his scandalous grace, and it all feels pretty good.

Resources

National Suicide Prevention Lifeline
1-800-273-TALK (8255)
Veteran's Crisis Line
1-800-273-TALK (8255) Press 1
Text Message Help
838255

TTY Services for Hearing Impaired
1-800-799-4889

www.veteranscrisisline.net

www.suicidepreventionlifeline.org

Alcoholics Anonymous
www.aa.org

Narcotics Anonymous
www.na.org

Contact your local Vet Center for more resources

To connect with Meredith Shafer, go
to www.meredithshafer.com

Made in the USA
San Bernardino, CA
12 October 2018